James Baird McClure

Mistakes of Ingersoll

As shown by Rev. W.F. Crafts, Bishop Charles E. Cheney and other: including Ingersoll's lecture on Skulls, and his answer to Prof. Swing and other critics

James Baird McClure

Mistakes of Ingersoll

As shown by Rev. W.F. Crafts, Bishop Charles E. Cheney and other: including Ingersoll's lecture on Skulls, and his answer to Prof. Swing and other critics

ISBN/EAN: 9783337307776

Printed in Europe, USA, Canada, Australia, Japan

Cover: Foto ©Lupo / pixelio.de

More available books at **www.hansebooks.com**

MISTAKES

OF

INGERSOLL

AS SHOWN BY

Rev. W. F. Crafts, Bishop Charles E. Cheney, Chaplain C. C.
McCabe, D.D., Arthur Swazey, D.D., Robert Collyer, D.D.,
Fred. Perry Powers, and Others.

INCLUDING INGERSOLL'S LECTURE

ON

SKULLS, AND HIS ANSWER

TO

Prof. Swing, Dr. Ryder, Dr. Herford, Dr. Collyer,
Dr. Thomas, Dr. Kohler, and Other Critics.

EDITED BY

J. B. McCLURE.

CHICAGO:
RHODES & McCLURE, PUBLISHERS.
1879.

PREFACE.

Not satisfied with his recent parade of the "Mistakes of Moses" before the Chicago public (which called forth our first book, entitled the "Mistakes of Ingersoll, as Shown By Prof. Swing and Others"), Mr. I. has since returned and delivered another lecture against the Bible and against his critics, Prof. Swing, Dr. Ryder, Dr. Herford and Dr. Collyer. These last efforts of Mr. Ingersoll have called forth the present volume, in which will be found additional "Mistakes," as shown by Rev. W. F. Crafts, who is the well-known successor of Dr. Tiffany in Trinity Methodist Episcopal Church; by Chaplain C. C. McCabe, Bishop Cheney, Arthur Swazey, D.D., Robert Collyer, D.D., whose names are all familar to the public; and by Fred Perry Powers, who is favorably identified with Chicago journalism. The "commendable fairness," mentioned by the press, in printing both the "text and replies" in the former volume, requires in this instance, also the text, which is given at the close and which includes Mr. Ingersoll's replies to Prof. Swing, Dr. Ryder, Brooke Herford and others.

J. B. McCLURE.

CHICAGO, May 17, 1879.

Entered according to Act of Congress, in the year 1879, by J. B. McCLURE & R. S. RHODES, in the Office of the Librarian of Congress, at Washington, D. C.

OTTAWAY & COMPANY, Printers.

DONOHUE & HENNEBERRY, Binders.

	PAGE
W. F. CRAFTS' REPLY	7
Ingersollism Outlined—"Ten Points" instead of "Five"—Infidel Protoplasm	7
First Point in the Ten—Sepulchral Hoots of the Ingersoll Owl—A Theological Rip Van Winkle	10
Ingersoll Mistakes a Part for the Whole—Gross Misrepresentations	12
The Great Ingersoll Boomerang—How it Works—Further Misrepresentations Examined	13
Misrepresenting Bible Passages	14
Sun and Moon Standing Still	15
Hell	16
The Present vs. the Future	17
Ingersoll's Horrible Estimate of Truth	19
The Bible the Best of Books, and Christ the Best of Men	20
Something New if True—Infidelity the Essential Factor in Progressive Civilization—But Coleridge, Wm. H. Seward, Bismarck, and other Great Statesman can not see it—Civilization goes only with Christianity	21
Marvelous Power of Time and Circumstance—Tragic Effect of Isothermal Lines—Peoria Mud Necessarily the Seventh Heaven as Ingersoll Sees it	24
Law is Ingersoll's God	26
Liberty and Infidelity—What De Tocqueville Says About it	26
Woman—Ingersoll's Theory at Variance with Facts	27
Ingersoll's Theory of Childhood—Some of His Little Stories—The Whole Subject Carefully Examined—Significant Incident in the Life of Abraham Lincoln	28
Ingersoll Says Christianity Fetters Thought—The Bible and a Host of Distinguished Men Say Otherwise	32
A Cloud of Witnesses	34
Jesus Christ	37
Amazing Ignorance of Infidels Concerning the Scriptures—Hume's Ignorance of the New Testament—Tom Paine Without a Bible	38

Distributed Ignorance and Concentrated Hatred—Probable Cause of Ingersoll's Infidelity 39
The Truth of the Whole Matter . 40

CHAPLAIN MCCABE'S REPLY 43
The Famous Chaplain Has a Remarkable Dream—He Sees the Great City of Ingersollville—Which Ingersoll and the Infidel Host Enter—And are Shut in for Six Months—Remarkable Condition of Things Outside and Inside—Happiness and Misery—Ingersoll Finally Petitions for a Church and sends for a Lot of Preachers 43

DR. SWAZEY'S REPLY 49
Momentary View of Col. Ingersoll Through the Doctor's Glass—The Bible on the Meridian—What the Doctor Sees in the Great Book 49
Occultation of Ingersoll's Good Sense—General Survey of Deities—Scope of Divine Revelation . . . 51
The Great Central Figure—Absolute Unity of the Bible System 53
The Bible Law of Development vs. Infidel Philosophy . 54
Common Sense View of the Subject—How it Eliminates Polygamy, Slavery, Etc. 56
More Common Sense—The Great Ingersoll Orb Approaching the Nihilistic Belt—Nebulæ 58

DR. COLLYER'S REPLY 63
Dr. Collyer Relates a Little Story—A Book that Cost Mr. Ingersoll the Governorship of Illinois—The Volume Philosophically Considered—Heavy Blows 63
Sparks Flying in all Directions—Singular Mental Phenomenon Occasioned by $25,000 a Year 64
The Clear Ring of Truth vs. the Dull Thud of the Baser Metal—Potency of Simple Statement—The Doctor's Objections to Ingersoll's Talk 67
Putting the Fine Edge on Orthodoxy—Taking a Weld with Prof. Swing and Dr. Thomas—Borax and Bigotry . . 69
A Touching Illustration—Eloquence and Truth—Havelock's Saints 73
Atheism—Not an Institution but a "Destitution!"—The True Life 74

FRED. PERRY POWERS' REPLY 75
The Sinaitic Code—Solvent Powers of the Historic Method—Graphic Illustration of the Two Schools . . . 75

CONTENTS.

Divine Adjustment of the Moral Law—Progressive Elimination of Polygamy, Slavery, Etc.—Mount Sinai and Mount Calvary ... 78
Purpose and Potency of the Mosaic Law ... 80
Excessive Wickedness and Proportionate Punishment—The Court of Heaven vs. the Court of Earth ... 82
Able Bodied Mendacity and Civilization—Love and Obedience ... 84
Mr. Powers' Pungent Peroration ... 85

BISHOP CHENEY'S REPLY ... 89
How the Question of Forgery Applies to the Five Books of Moses ... 89
The "Common Ground" of the Contending Parties—Logical Position of Ezra ... 91
The Bishop Planting Signals on the Mountain Tops of History—Survey of the New Moses Air Line ... 92
Termination of the Great Air Line ... 95
Genealogical Reflections, ... 96
Cutting the Gordian Knot ... 97
The Bishop's Challenge—Moses and Ingersoll as Chronologists ... 98
Mud Calendars vs. Facts—Some Sad and Sorrowful Scientific Figuring in the Sand ... 101
A Mistake of Ingersoll, Tom Paine & Co. Corrected—Conclusion ... 103

INGERSOLL'S LECTURE ON SKULLS and his Replies to Prof. Swing, Dr. Ryder, Dr. Herford, Dr. Collyer, and Other Critics, ... 107

MISTAKES OF INGERSOLL

AS SHOWN BY

W. F. CRAFTS,	ROBERT COLLYER, D. D.
CHAPLAIN McCABE,	F. P. POWERS,
ARTHUR SWAZEY, D. D.	BISHOP CHENEY,

AND OTHERS.

ALSO INCLUDING

INGERSOLL'S LECTURE IN FULL ON "SKULLS," AND HIS REPLIES TO PROF. SWING, W. H. RYDER. BROOKE HERFORD. AND OTHER CRITICS.

W. F. CRAFTS' REPLY.

Ingersollism Outlined—"Ten Points" instead of "Five"—Infidel Protoplasm.

"I war with principles, not with men"—the motto of Webster in political debates—should be the law in all conflicts of ideas, especially in the realm of religion. It is not of the person, Mr. Ingersoll, that I speak, but rather of the principles of which he is the most popular spokesman, and which make up that shallowest, but loudest, Jericho book of infidelity's bitter waters which begins in a few tears of pretended martyrdom to love of truth; spatters the mud of epithets upon Christians, while condemning that very vice in a part of the Church in less advanced ages; babbles shallowly along its little channel about law as an almighty executive, as if the rails that give direction to a train took the place of the engine that draws it; winds very crookedly through the Old Testament, avoiding every passage except those few that can be used for ridicule; plows still more crookedly through church history, shunning every part except the unchristian swamps of bigotry and superstition; keeps up the same snaky crookedness in its passage through religion of to-day, hurrying noisily among only the few rocky and marshy places, where it can find the reptiles of superstition and error; passes with great dash of spray along the audacious theory that Christian civilization is the result of anti-Christian forces; plunges with loud roar of waters down its claim that infidelity is the only liberator of man, woman, and child; and still flowing within its narrow little channel babbles of itself as an emancipated ocean of untrammeled thought.

These characteristics of the brook are the ten points of Ingersollism. I have read and re-read, carefully, the nine published lectures of Mr. Ingersoll on religious themes, besides hearing the one entitled "Skulls," and every one of them has something on each of these ten points of his fixed and unchanging creed, and not one or all has anything beyond these ten "doctrines"—for he often uses the words, "That is my doctrine." While attacking creeds of the Church he holds and urges all to believe his own unformulated but distinct creed, offering in place of the "five points of Calvinism" the ten points of Ingersollism, the latter occurring as regularly in every one of his lectures in this age as the former did a century ago in the sermons of Calvinists, which he ridicules for their sameness.

What is this frightful monster that we call "a creed?" Simply a statement of what one believes. Every man, unless he is an idiot, has a creed in which he agrees with somebody. The only question is to find by "reason, observation, and experience," which is the best. It would hardly be considered bigotry for a scientist to believe a few things as a creed of fixed scientific truths which no progress can ever erase, for instance, the rotundity and revolution of the earth, the attraction of the planets upon each other, and scores of other things which every scientist has held for many years unchanged, and is sure are unchangeable because proved conclusively. There are some certainties in the science of religion, such as are referred to in the Apostles' Creed, which may, without any greater bigotry, be considered as proved and established. The Christian Church of to-day does not generally insist upon anything further than these few concrete facts of the Apostles' Creed "as essentials" in Christian belief. When Evangelical churches shout their watchword, "In essentials, unity; in non-essentials, liberty; in all things, charity," it is as if a company of scientists should say, "On proved facts we will all agree, but in the realms of hypothesis and opinion, we will agree to disagree."

But the special point we wish to notice is, that Mr. Ingersoll attacks creed with creed. He is as bigoted a partisan of his own creed as ever called hard names. The very heart of his creed seems to be the belief that his mission is to destroy the creed of everybody else.

It is a suggestive fact that the naturally-gifted mind of Mr. Ingersoll, who declares that godless and soulless materialism is the emancipator and inspirer of thought, should be able, in all the years which these ten lectures represent, to produce but ten ideas, the same ten ideas which made up his earliest lecture, years ago, appearing successively in each of the succeeding lectures, including that of to-day, there being no change save in the cap and bells of his jokes. Reading these ten ideas over and over for as many hours in going through these lectures, brought back a ludicrous scene in our college burial of mathematics when fifteen notes of Pleyel's hymn were played dolefully over and over again for nearly an hour, as marching music.

In reading these lectures, which are but ten combinations and permutations of ten ideas, one is reminded also of the lecturer's own illustration of the boarding house keeper, who, for years, had no change of diet from hash, for every lecture is the same hash of ten ideas, changed only in the name and in the order of putting in the ten elements.

ARTICLE I.

First Point in the Ten—Sepulchral Hoots of the Ingersoll Owl— A Theological Rip Van Winkle.

As in the beet hash of New England the blood red beet predominates and gives color to the whole, so the principal element in these lectures against Christianity is the blood of past persecutions by a corrupt part of the Church, for which true Christianity has no more responsibility than a loyal colonel in our war of 1776, or 1861, for the robberies and crimes of camp-followers or traitors. In every published lecture on religion, Mr. Ingersoll deliberately cites the acts of the Benedict Arnolds of the Christian army as representing the Washingtons and Grants. He describes past counterfeits of religion as specimens of its accepted currency. It is as if one should attack present astronomers by relating ridiculous stories of the old astrologers, or assail present physicians by quoting the strange practices of the ancient alchemists.

In one lecture—a fair representative of all in this respect —I found that in forty-three pages only two did not contain these stale references to past persecutions, except a few pages given to the trial of Professor Swing, which were equally stale as assailing chiefly abandoned features of human Calvinism. Past errors and follies of the human Calvinism, human Catholicism, and heathen religions are constantly spoken of as if vital elements of Christianity.

Mr. Ingersoll ought to have a hymn to sing at the opening and close of his lectures, made on the pattern of that one whose first verse is:

> Go on, go on, go on, go on,
> Go on, go on, go on,
> Go on, go on, go on, go on,
> Go on, go on, go on,

with forty-two verses more of the same, substituting " past persecutions," instead of " go on," which is too progressive for a " go-back " lecture.

Mr. Ingersoll is a Rip Van Winkle in theology, who seems to have slept ever since the days of persecution. He is a Sancho Panza who assails imaginary foes of his own making, and thinks he has captured the golden helmet of Christianity when he has only secured the abandoned brass kettle of old traditions and discarded superstitions. He is a Falstaff killing the dead Percy of past follies. His lectures bustle with the antiquated and misused words "priests," " dark ages," " witches," " fagots," " religious wars," " church fathers," " damned infants," " martyrs," " gods," etc., as if he were speaking in a heathen land, and also in some dead century. And he uses the past tense so exclusively in his " progressive " lectures that one would suppose English as well as Hebrew had no present tense. It must have been Mr. Ingersoll, in his boyhood, that came from his first hunt crying, " I've shot a cherub," having mistaken an owl for a cherub, because of the wretched pictures of the latter on the old grave stones. Mr. Ingersoll logically destroys some Church owl of the dark ages, and because it corresponds with his own caricature of the Church thinks he has dethroned Christianity itself. Like Poe's "raven" who had but one word, "Nevermore." Mr. Ingersoll is continually crying in the ears of the present that worn-out strain about abuses which we all condemn, "Galileo-Servetus, Galileo-Servetus."

This ten-idea champion of popular materialism, while talking of progress and condemning those who hold fast to things of the past, is nevertheless so largely devoted to showing his carefully preserved martyr-mummies from the long-past ages of persecution, that we find Mark Twain's question constantly arising at each new charge against Christianity: "Is he—is he dead?" and we are also tempted to cry out for a "fresh corpse" in place of these very dry and dead mummies of past abuses. To paraphrase the lecturer's own words, we want one present fact. We pass our hats through the lectures in vain for some present facts against pure Christianity, which he assumes to assail and overthrow. There is far more excuse for Thomas Paine, in an age when the old Calvinistic errors were largely held, and for Voltaire, surrounded by the superstitions of Romanism, misunderstanding Christianity, than for this modern lecturer, who very well knows that the caricatures which he represents as Christianity are very old pictures of its ancient camp-followers.

ARTICLE II.

Ingersoll Mistakes a Part for the Whole—Gross Misrepresentations.

Article Second of Ingersollism, like unto the first, but with present instead of past tense, is about as follows: Christianity to-day is proved to be false by the present errors and abuses that are found in some of the churches.

Romish superstitions and the errors of those who have grossly misinterpreted the Bible as a support of slavery, polygamy, etc., are continually used by this champion of "liberty of thought," and "charity" and "brotherhood," as representing true Christianity to-day, which is quite as honorable as if a man should attack the principles of medicine by citing the tricks of quacks. An examination of the hull of the Great Eastern found adhering to the iron-plates of the bottom an enormous multitude of mussels, whose weight is estimated at three hundred tons. The great ship has been carrying on her hull a burden equal to full cargoes for six or eight sailing ships.

Suppose I should show you a few of those barnacles as specimens of what the Great Eastern is made of, and then denounce its builders as fools? Mr. Ingersoll is constantly confounding barnacles of some "church" with Christianity. Suppose I should take the belts and whips of torture that are used by Romanists in Mexico and show them in lectures as specimens of the barbarism of Congregationalists and Methodists? It is certainly most palpable unfairness for Mr. Ingersoll to use the word "gods" indiscriminately of heathen and Christian objects of worship, and to employ the words, "The Church," as if there were no false or true, past or present in connection with it, and as if its meaning were as much a unit as "The Moon." So also he unfairly classes all ministers as "priests." It would be quite as fair to speak of all "medicine men," past and present, savage and civilized, under the words, "The Doctors."

ARTICLE III.

The Great Ingersoll Boomerang—How it Works—Further Misrepresentations Carefully Examined.

Far less prominent, but ever present, is the third element in Ingersollism—an oft-recurring moan—"Infidels to-day are martyrs at whom men cast epithets, but not ballots."

The defeated infidel politician appears as regularly and

revengefully in every lecture (indirectly, of course) as the misanthropic Byron shows himself in each of his poems as the real hero under the various names of "Childe Harold" "Don Juan," "Corsair," etc. He who cries out against the past for calling infidels by hard names hurls in the more kindly present more anathemas than any other Pope.

"You are an infidel."

"You're a bigot! Arn't you ashamed to be calling names, you old hypocrite?"

In this debate of Mr. Ingersoll's bigotry with the bigotry of the past, a printer might fitly misprint the "pros and cons," "pigs and cows." It is like the English lady who criticised an American friend for saying, at a mistake in croquet, "What a horrid scratch," and when asked what would have been better, replied, "You might have said, 'What a beastly fluke.'" It is not strange that the people will not elect to represent them in politics, one who so audaciously misrepresents them, as does Mr. Ingersoll in nearly every attempt to declare the belief of Christians.

Misrepresenting Bible Passages.

Dr. Ryder, Prof. Swing, and Dr. Herford, have abundantly shown his numerous and inexcusable misrepresentations of Bible passages, to which may be added another more atrocious, if possible, the implication that the persecutions of Saul of Tarsus, and the adulteries of Solomon, are a part of the Christian system, and also that Jephthah really killed his daughter as a sacrifice, which the Bible does not declare, nor any Christian believe, and the misinterpretation of the passage about women keeping silence in the churches, which the Christian Church of to-day considers of only temporary force, a command to Corinth, and not to Christendom, no more binding upon us than Paul's request that Timothy should bring his cloak that was left at Troas. It is a kindred misrepresentation to say the assertion that those who tortured the martyrs were the same ones who made the Bible—an assertion which history clearly refutes, as the Old Testament was arranged in its present form 388 B. C., and the New Testament was collected as it is at present before the days of persecution by the church began.

It is also a misrepresentation, not only of the Bible, but of the common principles of interpretation in every department of literature, to intimate that an explanation of passages as poetic and figurative, is unfair and begging the question. Suppose we should put a literal interpretation upon the tropical figures of Mr. Ingersoll's eloquence, and when he speaks of the sun's rays "as arrows from the quiver of the sun," declare him an ignorant idolator, who thinks the sun an intelligent being who has caught the passion for archery.

Sun and Moon Standing Still.

It is equally absurd for him to interpret the poem about the sun and moon standing still by the rules of prose. Mr. Ingersoll also says, poetically: "Think of that wonderful chemistry by which bread was changed into the divine tragedy of Hamlet." Suppose we should interpret that sentence as fact rather than figure, and say that Mr. Ingersoll believes that by the combination of certain liquids and solids in the chemist's retort this marvelous literary production was created! It would be quite as reasonable as to insist upon absolute literalness in the bold figures of Oriental eloquence and poetry.

Mr. Ingersoll also misrepresents the Christian's Sunday in the home, speaking of it as "a day too good for a child to be happy in," saying: "The idea, that any God would hate to hear a child laugh." We all know (?) that in the

Christian homes of to-day the smiles and laughter of childhood are strictly forbidden, and any one who smiles in church is carried out by the police (?).

Hell.

Especially does Mr. Ingersoll continually and grossly misrepresent Christianity in regard to the conditions by which men are believed to bring themselves to Hell. Hear him: "It is infinitely absurd to suppose that a God would address a communication to intelligent beings, and yet make it a crime, to be punished in eternal flames, for them to use their intelligence for the purpose of understanding His communication. Neither can they show why any one should be punished, either in this world or another, for acting honestly in accordance with reason; and yet a doctrine with every possible argument against it has been, and still is, believed and defended by the entire orthodox world. If I should say ninety-nine in a hundred go down to Hell, I should have the support of the entire orthodox world. You can see for yourselves the justice of damning a man if his parents happened to baptize him in the wrong way. Think of a God who will damn his children for the expression of an honest thought!"

Few, if any, intelligent Christians teach that a man must accept their denominational creed in all its details in order to be saved, as the careless critics of Christianity so often assert, but rather all evangelical Christians repeat the New Testament conditions of salvation, "Believe on the Lord Jesus Christ and thou shalt be saved," and declare negatively, not as has been said by Mr. Ingersoll, said by infidels, that all who do not believe will not be saved, but rather in the words of Martin Luther, "No man shall die in his sins, except him who, through disbelief, thrusts from him the forgiveness of sin, which in the name of Jesus is offered him." It is the firm of Ignorance and Bigotry that declare that evangelical Christianity teaches that a man can not be saved who does not believe in its statement of the Trinity and its interpretations of the Bible.

He also utterly misrepresents the Christian conception of saving faith as ignoring reason and action, both of which it includes, and as resting chiefly on a book or a creed as its end, rather than on the person, Christ. Every church teaches that intelligent faith and faithfulness toward Christ (not creeds in detail) is the condition of salvation. "Faith," says Bishop Wightman, "believes on competent testimony what it could not otherwise know." Or, as Dr. Arnold says: "Faith is reason leaning on God." Reason is the foundation of belief.

The Present vs. the Future.

Another of the almost countless misrepresentations of religion by Mr. Ingersoll, is the frequent statement that Christianity is wholly devoted to the future, and ignores man's present needs, which reminds us that it was Thomas Paine (?) and not the Bible that said, "Pure religion and undefiled before God the Father, is this, to visit the fatherless and the widows in their affliction, and to keep himself unspotted from the world." And you have all observed that the organized societies and benevolences, by which orphans, and the aged, and the helpless, are aided in asylums and refuges, were not (?) established by this Christianity which "ignores man's present needs, and devotes itself exclusively to the future." Christian ministers never preach on combining works with faith, or showing character by conduct, or loving their neighbors as themselves. Mr. Ingersoll declares that a little restitution is better than a great deal of repentance, and we have noticed that when Ingersoll has delivered a lecture or two in our large cities, those among his hearers who have defrauded others have, at once, begun the work of restitution (?) by sending back the money they had stolen from employers, creditors and customers. (?) Mr. Moody, who preaches repentance as well as restitution, of course (?) has no such results following his work, as he proclaims the Christianity whose entire interest is in the future life. (?) You smile at this practical test of Mr. Ingersoll's theory, in view of the fact that we have no record of a single instance where one of his lectures has led to the restitution of stolen property; while such cases are constantly occurring in connection with the work of Mr. Moody and other Christians. Several very notable ones have come under my own immediate notice.

It is an equally astounding, barefaced misrepresentation, or to put it in fewer letters, false, when he states that all of the orthodox religion of the day is Calvinistic. Part of the so-called Calvinistic churches are not Calvinistic in the usual sense of the word, and we had fondly dreamed that there was such a body of Christians as Methodists who are distinctly anti-Calvinistic, and hold the first place in numbers among Protestant Churches in America.

It is also a misrepresentation to say, "Whoever thinks he has found it all out, he is orthodox," for every orthodox pulpit constantly preaches the duty of growth, intellectual and spiritual. Mr. Ingersoll declares that Protestants to-day would persecute, as in the past, if they had the power, a statement in which he assumes the role of the prophet, and shows the profundity of his insight into the spirit of Christianity to-day, which binds up the broken-hearted and ministers to the troubled and sorrowing. It is cunning sophistry to say that every one is opposed to the union of Church and state, because they know that the Church could not be trusted with power, a statement which obtains its force by suppressing the very important fact that the

Church when united with political power draws into itself unprincipled politicians, and becomes entirely a different body through the opportunities it offers to selfishness and ambition. It is also a misrepresentation to say that " Protestants stand up for Protestant persecutors of the past," for all Protestant churches of to-day condemn the burning of Servetus and such acts as much as any one. It is also a misrepresentation by holding back half the truth to tell us of that base or mistaken element of the Church that made the rack and not of that other noble element of the Church that was upon the rack, for the martyrs were seldom if ever infidels.

Ingersoll's Horrible Estimate of Truth.

Mr. Ingersoll, in his recent lecture on " Skulls," twice said that truth was not worth a little suffering, that one had better lie or recant than suffer a little pain, or lose a drop of blood. He would " turn Judas Iscariot to his own soul " to save a thumb. This significant item as to his whole estimate of truth helps us to account for the wholesale manufacture of falsehoods in his lectures.

Mr. Ingersoll's most gross misrepresentation is the habitual custom of telling only one side of a fact, quoting difficult Bible passages but never sublime ones, bad customs of the Church but never good ones. defects in Christians but never excellences. When Mr. Ingersoll speaks of " a lawyer whipping his child for holding back part of the truth," he describes his own partisan and one-sided method, as Professor Swing has shown, attacking Christianity as the hired attorney of infidelity, or the hired campaigner of the anti-Christian party who is to present only one side. This, too, from a man who claims that infidelity unfetters thought and broadens mind.

The Bible the Best of Books, and Christ the Best of Men.

Mr. Ingersoll also misrepresents the differences among the various forms of Christianity. All men of broad scholarship of the last and best century who have written on religion, both skeptics and Christians, agree on two things—the Bible as the best of books, and Christ as the best of men. So much at least may be said to be indorsed by all scholarship, and when a man rests down upon these two truths as proved and established, and follows them out into the truths to which they lead, he will not be likely to go far astray, for if Christ is confessedly the greatest and best of men, the "Teacher sent from God," then His teachings are to be accepted, and those teachings are the foundations of all essential Christianity; and if the Bible is the best of books, the moral and spiritual guide of man, then its teachings are to be carefully read and deeply regarded, and all who take this book as life's guide book will be led into all truths of Christianity that are fundamental and important.

All Christians, Romanists and Protestants, agree that Christ is the living embodiment and pattern of Christian manhood, and that the Bible, at least, contains the "Word of God." All evangelical Christians agree on that broad and simple platform of the Apostles Creed, and declare not "many," but one way to Heaven, and that not by "believing an incomprehensible creed." but by faith and faithfulness of intellect, will, heart and life, toward the person, Jesus Christ. Two quotations fairly represent all the evangelical churches on this matter. Bishop Whipple, an Episcopalian, recently remarked, "As the grave grows nearer, my theology is growing strangely simple, and it begins and ends with Christ, as the only refuge for the lost." Dr. Alexander, of Princeton, a Presbyterian, when dying said; "All my theology is reduced to this narrow compass, 'Jesus Christ came into the world to save sinners.'" Mr. Ingersoll, misrepresents the most familiar facts when he says, "Just in proportion as the human race has advanced, the church has lost power. There is no exception to this rule." It is a fact so familiar that every intelligent child knows it, that Christianity was never so powerful in the world, as to-day—never had so many followers. By the multiplied agencies of church work, six thousand are converted per day—two Pentecosts every twenty-four hours.

Mr. Ingersoll misrepresents not only the Bible and church history, by leaving out all that would not help his theories, and stating one half the truth, but he also misrepresents the Declaration of Independence as "retiring God from politics," as if the words were not there, "the station to which the laws of nature, and nature's God entitle them," "All men are endowed by their Creator with certain inalienable rights"—"and for the support of this declaration, and in a firm reliance upon Divine Providence, we mutually pledge to each other our lives, our fortunes, and our sacred honor." It is surely infinitely absurd to expect a man broadly and truly to represent us in politics, who so inexcusably and grossly misrepresents us in religion.

ARTICLE IV.

Something New if True—Infidelity the Essential Factor in Progressive Civilization—But Coleridge, Wm. H. Seward, Bismarck, and other great Statesmen can not see it— Civilization goes only with Christianity.

The fourth article in Ingersollism is as follows: "The civilization of this country is not the child of faith, but of unbelief—the result of free thought. But for the efforts of a few brave infidels, the church would have taken the world back to the midnight of barbarism." How ignorant we have all been! Luther, who led Europe out of the Dark Ages, was not, it seems, a child of faith, but of free thought (?) and Paul also, who brought civilization into barbarous Europe, peopled with savage tribes, as described by Julius Cæsar in his Commentaries. The transformation of savage Gaul and Britain into civilized France and England was accomplished by the efforts of "unbelief." (?)

Long ago, Christianity had a contest with Atheism, Pantheism, and Culture, as to which was the best civilizer. Christianity selected Europe, and gave the other three contestants Asia, with several centuries the start. Atheism, or Buddhism, which ignores all spiritual things and devotes itself to the present life, has operated for thousands of years in India. Pantheism, or Brahminism, made its experiment in the same country; and Culture obtained exclusive control of China, ruling both church and state. As a result, in accordance with Mr. Ingersoll's theory, these elements of Ingersollism have developed a lofty civilization (?) in China and India, given education to woman, torn away the veil of her slavish seclusion, made her the equal of man, treated female infants as honorably as the boys, developed a high morality in the community, and supplied the world with its standard literature, its foremost science, and its chief inventions.(?) On the other hand, Christianity came into barbarous Europe a dozen centuries later, caused the degradation and enslavement of women and children, (?) repressed scientific investigation. (?) prevented invention, (?) checked thought, (?) and thus hindered literary activity, and, by the barbarism of the Bible, "brought bondage to man, woman, and child" in body and brain.(?) If the facts do not correspond to these legitimate deductions from Mr. Ingersoll's theories as to the effect of atheistic culture, on the one hand, and Christianity, on the other, upon national life, so much the worse for the facts.

Mr. Ingersoll says much against the wars of Christian nations. He forgets that peace societies and arbitration were never known outside of Christianity, and that wars in Christian lands are the gradually disappearing remains of previous barbarism. He talks of science and invention as opening up this era! How does it happen that all this is in Christian rather than in heathen lands? He talks of charity and benevolence of infidels! Why is it that all benevolent societies are Christian, and that Thomas Paine halls can not be supported? He talks of liberty of speech and thought and government! Why is it that such liberty is only found in Christian countries? He has much to say of the barbarous age of dug-outs, tom-toms, and wooden plows! Has he not seen in the World's Expositions these very things as representing nations to-day, that have not risen from their primitive degradation and ignorance because Christianity has not yet reached them?

As to the relation of the Bible to civilization, Samuel Taylor Coleridge declares that "for more than a thousand years the Bible, collectively taken, has gone hand in hand with civilization, science, law, in short, with moral and intellectual cultivation, always supporting, and often leading the way."

William H. Seward says, "The whole hope of human progress is suspended on the ever-growing influence of the Bible."

Bismarck utters a similar sentiment, as quoted in his recent biography: "How, without faith in a revealed religion, in a God who wills what is good, in a Supreme Judge, and a future life, men can live together harmoniously —each doing his duty and letting every one else to do his— I do not understand." Similar sentiments are uttered by the leading statesmen of all lands, the unanimous verdict of statesmanship being that civilization can not be carried forward without Christianity.

ARTICLE V.

Marvelous Power of Time and Circumstance—Tragic Effect of Iso-thermal Lines—Peoria Mud Necessarily the Seventh Heaven as Ingersoll Sees it.

The fifth article of Ingersollism is, that gods and men are but evolutions of matter and circumstance, the difference between heathen gods and the Christian's God being the result of a difference in their worshippers, and the difference in men being the result of varying soils and surroundings. He says: "No god was ever in advance of the nation that created him." In answer to this last statement, which is true, of course, of all imaginary deities, but not of the One True God, it is only necessary to ask any candid and intelligent man to read the description of God given in the Bible, where both Testaments declare Him to be "merciful and gracious, long suffering and abundant in goodness and truth, but will by no means spare the guilty," and then say whether this God is nothing more than the reflection of the stiff-necked and perverse people who held to this conception of Deity. The fact is, God as described in the Bible is infinitely loftier and purer than the Jewish people, or any people of any age. It is still more absurd, if possible, for Mr. Ingersoll to assert that "men are but the creatures of their surroundings, made what they are wholly by material causes, such as soil and climate." It is one of the characteristic contradictions of history, such as are found so frequently in Mr. Ingersoll's lectures, when he asserts that great minds have never been found except in the "lands of respectable winters," with the intimation that no great achievements in art or literature are possible in warm

Oriental lands. As if Babylon, and Nineveh, and Egypt had not been in early ages the universities of the world. Carlyle must have been very much deceived when he declared Job of the Oriental land of Uz to be the greatest poet the world has known. Mohammed of those warm lands was certainly great, even though wrong, and scores of others, equally eminent, might be mentioned, although, of course, it is evident that greatness of men or peoples in tropical lands is rather in spite of circumstances than by their help.

Mr. Ingersoll in his lecture on "Man, Woman, and Child," speaking of one of these warm countries as the representative of all, says: "You might go there with five thousand Congregational preachers, five thousand deacons, five thousand professors in colleges, five thousand of the solid men of Boston and their wives, settle them all, and you will see the second generation riding upon a mule bareback, no shoes, a grapevine whip, with a rooster under each arm going to a cock fight on Sunday. Such is the influence of climate." But like most of Mr. Ingersoll's theories, this one is unfortunately the direct opposite of facts. The Sandwich Islands have all these disadvantages of climate, and fifty years ago were plunged in the deepest barbarism, with all the vices of savage life; but to-day, as all well-informed persons know, they are as truly civilized as any land, with industries, education, protection of life and property, equal to what is found in our own favored country. And this is all due, as King Kalikua said in New York, to the Christianizing of his people. Indeed, Mr. Ingersoll contradicts his own theory as to the dependence of the individual upon surroundings in his lectures on Humboldt and Paine, both of whom he represents as becoming great in spite of surroundings that would naturally have led in the opposite direction, thus involuntarily recognizing something in man deeper than mere physical evolution.

The whole absurd theory of individuals and nations being wholly dependent upon soil, and climate, and surroundings for their character, is fairly represented in the following incident:

" Pa," said a little six-year old, " what makes me grow ?"

" Why, the bread and potato I feed you with."

" Does potatoes make our pig grow, too?"

" Yes."

" Then, what makes him be a pig and me be a boy?"

That boy's simple question explodes all the theories of evolution.

ARTICLE VI.
Law is Ingersoll's God.

The sixth article of Ingersollism is, " I believe in law, the Almighty maker of Heaven and earth." One might as well say that the United States Constitution made our country, or try to rule the land by laws without enforcers.

That the universe is governed according to a system of law is recognized by Christians as much as by any one, and the laws of the Bible are not new arbitrary enactments, but recognitions and proclamations of that part of the law-system of the universe that relates to religion and morality. Laws of spirit are as eternal as laws of matter. Natural science proclaims the latter, religious science the former.

ARTICLE VII.
Liberty and Infidelity—What De Tocqueville Says About it.

The seventh article is made up of the following statements: " All religions are inconsistent with mental freedom. The doubter, the investigator, the infidel, have been the saviours of liberty."

Mr. Ingersoll, when talking of liberty contradicts what he himself has said of law, and fails to remind his hearers and readers that the circle of law bounds on every side the privileges of liberty, that one has liberty only within the range of propriety, and that all beyond that is license. He also forgets the very evident fact that the prevailing ideas of personal liberty in the world are due to the general dissemination, by Christianity, of the truth that a man is a soul as well as a body. Wherever men are regarded as mere physical beings, with no life deeper than the bodily life, the stronger will enslave the weaker—woman, child and captive. When the idea that each man is an immortal soul takes hold upon man, with it there comes the idea of individual rights. If Ingersollism should ever persuade a civilized people that man has no soul, this form of bondage of the weaker to the stronger will be resumed. Not soil, but soul, is the secret of liberty.

Even Mr. Frothingham recently declared that the Bible is a democratic book, and that we get out of it our ideas of equality. He remembered what Mr. Ingersoll seems to forget, that all through the Bible, the idea of personal and religious liberty is found, especially in those words of the Apostles to the rulers who attempted to tyrannize over their consciences, "We ought to obey God rather than man," which has fitly been termed the concisest of all statements of the principles of personal liberty. We may show this relation of religion to liberty in the words of the greatest modern writer upon such questions, De Tocqueville, who says, "Bible Christianity is the companion of liberty in all its conflicts, the cradle of its infancy, and the divine source of its claims."

ARTICLE VIII.

Woman—Ingersoll's Theory at Variance with Facts.

The eighth article of Ingersollism, is in regard to woman, and is as follows: "As long as woman regards the Bible as the charter of her rights, she will be the slave of man.

The Bible was not written by a woman. Within its lids there is nothing but humiliation and shame for her."

You have all doubtless observed that in heathen countries, where the Bible has not yet come with its enslaving (?) influence woman has (?) liberty and honor, and education, and opportunities of public activity and benevolence (?), but in Christian lands she is veiled, degraded, shut out of sight and restrained from education (?). I have always observed, as a pastor, that it is the religious, and church-going husbands that tyrannize over their wives as "bosses," and deny them their liberties of conscience, and other rights. (?)

You smile at the absurd statement, knowing that the "heathen at home," who as husbands are harsh and brutal to the wives they have promised to cherish, are frequently ardent believers in Ingersollism, and seldom in any way connected with even nominal Christianity, while every school boy is familiar with the fact that woman, in all except Christian lands, is hardly better than a slave, notably so, in that land where Ingersollism under the name of Buddhism has the controlling influence. Mr. Ingersoll utters many true sentiments about the family, but all of these he learned of Christianity, not from China, or Egypt.

ARTICLE IX.

Ingersoll's Theory of Childhood—Some of His Little Stories—The Whole Subject Carefully Examined—Significant Incident in the Life of Abraham Lincoln.

The ninth article of Ingersollism is a theory of childhood which attacks the principles of sound government and health even more than religion: "Do not have it in your mind that you must govern them; that they (children) must obey. Let your children eat what they desire. They know what they wish to eat. Let them begin at which end of the dinner they please."

Such a theory is worthy of nothing more than the smile with which you hear it. It is all answered in the following representative fact of childhood: A little bit of a girl wanted more and more buttered toast, till she was told that too much would make her sick. Looking wistfully at the dish for a moment, she thought she saw a way out of her difficulty, and exclaimed, "Well, give me annuzer piece, and send for the doctor!"

Mr. Ingersoll, in connection with his theory of childhood, often refers to the fact, that he leaves his pocket-book around where his children can help themselves to whatever they wish, and urges the same course upon all parents. It is said that one of the lecturer's admirers, being convinced that this was the correct theory, determined to give up punishing his child, and try the new plan. Accordingly, he said to his boy, "John, I am convinced I have been taking the wrong course to try to make you a better boy. I am going to trust you more, and give up whippings. I am going away for a few days, and I have left my pocket-book in the top drawer of the bureau. Help yourself to money whenever you need it." After a few days the father returned to his home, late at night. As he opened the door he stumbled over a large canoe in the entry, and was then attacked by a large bull-dog that his boy had bought. Entering the boy's room, he found it hung round with guns, and fishing poles, and daggers, with another canoe, and several small dogs—his pocket-book lying empty on the top of the bureau. He is now less enthusiastic in regard to Ingersoll's knowledge of domestic government.

The leading point which Mr. Ingersoll endeavors to make in connection with his lecture on Thomas Paine is that the Bible shocks a child, and, therefore, can't be true. You have all observed how much children are shocked as they gather about the mother's knees in the twilight, and hear her tell the stories of Jesus, and Joseph, and Moses, and Samuel, and Daniel (?). As to the relation of the Bible to childhood and home life, let me quote the opinion of several eminent men, mostly skeptics, for whom even Mr. Ingersoll cherishes the highest regard:

Thomas Jefferson, speaking of the Bible and home life, says: "I have always said, and always will say, that the studious perusal of the sacred volume will make better citizens, better fathers, and better husbands."

John Quincy Adams says: "So great is my veneration for the Bible, that the earlier my children begin to read it, the more confident will be my hopes that they will prove useful citizens to their country and respectable members of society."

Theodore Parker says: "There is not a boy on the hills of New England, not a girl born in the filthiest cellar which disgraces a capital in Europe, and cries to God against the barbarism of modern civilization; not a boy nor a girl all Christendom through, but their lot is made better by that great book."

Diderot, the French philosopher and skeptic, was wont to make this confession: "No better lessons than those of the Bible can I teach my child."

Huxley, in an address upon education, says: "I have always been strongly in favor of secular education, in the sense of education without theology; but I must confess I have been no less seriously perplexed to know by what practical measures the religious feeling, which is the essential basis of conduct, was to be kept up, in the present utterly chaotic state of opinion on these matters, without the use of the Bible. The pagan moralists lack life and color, and even the noble stoic, Marcus Aurelius, is too high and refined for an ordinary child. Take the Bible as a whole, make the severest deductions which fair criticism can dictate, and there still remains in this old literature a vast residuum of moral beauty and grandeur. By the study of what other book could children be so humanized? If Bible reading is not accompanied by constraint and solemnity, I do not believe there is anything in which children take more pleasure."

What would "shock the mind of a child" would be to hear Mr. Ingersoll excuse them for telling a lie, in order to escape a whipping. What would shock a child would be to hear Mr. Ingersoll uttering profanity

What would shock the mind of a child would be to hear Mr. Ingersoll telling to a crowded audience with a smile of approval the story of a boy's oath.

Speaking of swearing reminds me of that incident of Abraham Lincoln, whom Mr. Ingersoll calls "the grandest man ever President of the United States," who said to a person sent to him by one of the Senators, and who, in conversation, uttered an oath, "I thought the Senator had sent me a gentleman; I see I was mistaken. There is the door, and I bid you good-day." I hold in my hand the last report of the New York Society for the Prevention of Cruelty to Children. Of course, the bruised and beaten little ones, here described, were the victims of cruelty in Christian homes (?). Their fathers and mothers had taken too much religion (?), had become brutalized by reading the Bible (?), and hence abused the children by their own fireside until the law was compelled to interfere for their defense (?).

In my work as a member of the Citizen's League for the suppression of the sale of liquors to minors, I have noticed that this supreme cruelty to children—selling them in their immature years the liquors that make them self-destroyers, violators of the public peace, and candidates for drunkards' graves—is perpetrated by Christian men, not by the infidels who applaud so lustily at Mr. Ingersoll's lectures (?). Here I am reminded of the published report, which seems well authenticated, that Mr. Ingersoll in his childhood lived in one of those exceptional homes where nominal Christianity was combined with harshness, cruelty and bigotry. If so, this would be some slight excuse for his present conduct, were it not for the fact that maturer years have given him abundant opportunity to see the bright and sunny side of Christian gentleness in other homes. And there are no true homes that do not owe their existence to the influence of Christianity upon the family relation.

Having myself made childhood a special study for several years, I find that the degree of recognition given to the opinions and importance of childhood in various ages and countries, is exactly in proportion to the degree of Christianity there, children being scarcely noticed in heathen lands, either in poetry, or history, or ethics, while the Bible religion has always given childhood an exceedingly prominent place. All the attention given to the education and development of the little ones is but the starlight that shines down upon us from the manger of the God-child.

ARTICLE X.

Ingersoll Says Christianity Fetters Thought—The Bible and a Host of Distinguished Men Say Otherwise.

The tenth article of Ingersollism is the frequent assertion that Christianity fetters thought, while infidelity emancipates it, in such passages as these: "In all ages, reason has been regarded as the enemy of religion." "The gods dreaded education and knowledge then (in the time of the Garden of Eden) just as they do now." "For ages a deadly conflict has been waged by a few brave men of thought and genius, on the one side, and the great, ignorant, religious mass, on the other. The few have said: 'Think.' The many have said: 'Believe.'"

In order to ascertain what freedom and power of thought materialism had given to the mind of Mr. Ingersoll, I made special examination of the logic in the lecture on "The Gods," and found there, in a very short time, one or more specimens of all the fallacies laid down in the text-books of logic. "Waiter," said John Randolph, at a certain hotel, "if this is coffee, bring me tea; if this is tea, bring me coffee." And so we say, if this is the "power of thought," give us weakness.

Instead of the Bible forbidding us to think, as Ingersollism so often declares, it is full of ringing appeals to "reason," "think," "consider," "ponder," "prove all things."

Prov. 26:16: "The sluggard is wiser in his own conceit than seven men that can render a *reason*."

Eccl. 7:25: "I applied mine heart to know, and to search, and to seek out wisdom, and the *reason* of things, and to know the wickedness of folly, even of foolishness and madness."

Isa. 1:18: "Come now and let us *reason* together, saith the Lord; though your sins be as scarlet, they shall be as white as snow; though they be red like crimson, they shall be as wool."

Matt. 22:42: "What *think* ye of Christ?"

Acts 17:2: "Paul, as his manner was, went in unto them, and three Sabbath days *reasoned* with them out of the Scriptures."

Acts 18:4: "He *reasoned* in the synagogue every Sabbath, and persuaded the Jews and the Greeks."

Acts 19:19: "And he came to Ephesus, and left them there; but he himself entered into the synagogue and *reasoned* with the Jews."

Acts 24:25: "And as he *reasoned* of righteousness, temperance, and judgment to come, Felix trembled."

Rom. 12:1: "I beseech you therefore, brethren, by the mercies of God, that you present your bodies a living sacrifice, holy, acceptable unto God, which is your *reasonable* service."

Phil. 4:8: "Finally, brethren, whatsoever things are true, whatsoever things are honest, whatsoever things are just, whatsoever things are pure, whatsoever things are lovely, whatsoever things are of good report, if there be any virtue, and if there be any praise, *think on these things.*"

1 Thess. 5:21: "Prove all things; hold fast that which is good."

Let us look into biography, and make a practical test of this theory that the Bible fetters thought. If so, those who believe and love it will not be strong and leading thinkers. Let us apply the test in the ranks of science.

A Cloud of Witnesses.

Professor Benjamin Pierce, of Harvard College, has recently completed a very remarkable course of lectures at the Lowell Institute, Boston, on "Ideality in Science." Professor Pierce, who is now in his seventieth year, is, perhaps, the most eminent mathematical scholar in this country, and the author of some of the most profound investigations and speculations that have been made in the realm of astronomical science. This man of mighty thought must have been emancipated and inspired by infidelity (?). This scholar, whose mind may be supposed to feed on fact, holds an unquestioning faith in a personal God and the immortal life.

The late Professor Henry, of the Smithsonian Institute, was one of the broadest and best of scientific thinkers because infidelity gave him freedom of thought (?). No, he was a sweet-spirited Christian in his daily life.

Sir David Brewster, another eminent scientist, said of his Christian experience: "I have had this light for many years, and oh! how bright it is to me."

Professor Silliman, who is unsurpassed in his scientific

department, must also be classed under the head of "the ignorant religious mass," for he was another of the very many Christian scientists, whom the world has ignorantly(?) supposed a thinker, in spite of Mr. Ingersoll's theory of faith as being a mental bondage. He says: "I can truly declare that, in the study and exhibition of science to my pupils and fellow men, I have never forgotten to give all honor and glory to the infinite Creator—happy if I might be the honored interpreter of a portion of his works, and of the beautiful structure and beneficent laws discovered therein by the labors of many illustrious predecessors." We might add scores of others in each department of science, who have found no discord between the Word and world of God.

Who are the four greatest thinkers in the realm of statesmanship of this century? Daniel Webster, Gladstone, Thiers, and Bismarck. All of them, of course, are enabled to be thus broad and prominent as national thinkers by the power of infidelity (?). No, each one of them is most positive in his Christian belief.

Webster declares the grandest thought which ever entered his mind was that of "personal accountability to God."

Gladstone gives much of time and attention to religious writing.

Thiers says, in his last days: "I often invoke that God in whom I am happy to believe, who is denied by fools and ignorant people, but in whom the enlightened man finds his consolation and hope."

Bismarck is called, in derision, "the God-fearing man," in reference to his well-known religious principles. (Busch's Bismarck, p. 200).

We might add to these Charles Sumner, who called Christianity the "true religion" and "our faith," and whose speeches constantly recognize God and Christianity.

Who are the leading literary characters of the century? Victor Hugo, what of him? Did you ever read his chapter on prayer in Les Miserables, and his grand tribute to immortality, uttered as a rebuke to a company of French physicians, a few years ago? Moore—have you read his "Paradise and the Peri," the Gospel of repentance, and do you know him as the author of the hymn. "Come, ye Disconsolate?" Walter Scott—have you read his translation of "Dies Iræ," uttered so devoutly in his last days:

> "Oh! in that day, that dreadful day,
> When Heaven and earth shall pass away,
> Be Thou, oh Christ, the sinner's st y,
> When Heaven and earth shall pass away."

And Shakspeare, whom Mr. Ingersoll accounts one of the grandest of human minds, was great enough to believe in the Bible. And so Thackeray, Whittier, Dickens, Goldsmith, Longfellow, and Irving were intellectual believers in Christianity.

The following men, also lacking the freedom and power of thought that comes by materialism (?) became mentally so weak (?) that they declared, in varying terms, after reading largely in all departments of literature, that the Bible is the best book in the world: Sir Walter Scott, Sir William Jones, George Gilfillan, Milton, Pollok, Coleridge, Collins, Bacon, John Adams, Napoleon, James Freeman Clarke, Lange, Kitto, Robertson. And Channing put the Gospels where these others place the whole Bible—above all other literature.

The following persons strongly commend the Bible as a whole: Dr. Samuel Johnson, Carlyle, Dryden, Young, Cowper, Locke, Newton, Seward, Dawson, Franklin, John Quincy Adams, Bellows, Bartol, Theodore Parker, Rousseau, Guizot, Bunsen, Story, Webster, Diderot, Matthew Arnold, and Huxley.

The following persons among many others declare that they found in the Bible, not fetters for thought, but their strongest inspiration to thought : Daniel Webster, Fisher Ames, Mitchell, the Astronomer, Ruskin and Goethe.

It is evident that very many others might truly have said the same, including Theodore Parker and Mr. Frothingham and other skeptics, whose writings show plainly that they owe their beauties of style to a familiarity with the Bible.

Jesus Christ.

With these great men who have commended the Bible should be mentioned one who is confessed by Christians and skeptics the greatest and best of men, JESUS CHRIST, who used the Psalms as His prayer and hymn book, and always spoke of the whole Old Testament as the Eternal Law Book of humanity. There is not time, nor is it necessary now to answer in detail all the hard questions that can be asked about single Bible passages. But these great men and Christ saw all these points of difficulty, and yet accepted the Bible as the pre-eminent book, commending it to the perusal of all as the source of the mind's grandest inspirations. Side by side with these scores of the world's foremost men who declare the Bible the best of books, or strongly commend it, or point to it as the source of their grandest thoughts, put the opinion of that more learned (?), more profound (?), more unprejudiced (?) scholar and philosopher, Colonel Ingersoll, who stands almost alone among educated men in strongly condemning the Bible, which his bigotry prints with a small "b" in spite of the rules of grammar, and describes it as about the worst book of the world, in these words among others: "If men will read the Bible as they read other books, they will be amazed that they ever, for one moment, supposed a being of infinite wisdom to be the author of such ignorance and of such atrocity. The Bible burned heretics, built dungeons, founded the inquisition, and trampled upon all the liberties of men. All the philosophy of the Bible would not make one scene in Hamlet. I could write a better book than the Bible, which is full of barbarism."

Amazing Ignorance of Infidels Concerning the Scriptures—Hume's Ignorance of the New Testament—Tom Paine Without a Bible.

" But some one asks, Are there not other eminent men who have despised and condemned the Bible? Most certainly, as there are those who have entered their protest against almost any and everything mentionable. It is, nevertheless, worthy of note that, in most instances, those who have sought the more resolutely to defame the Holy Scriptures are those who are comparatively unacquainted with them. David Hume, distinguished both as essayist and historian, standing among the most noted of modern skeptical philosophers, was a resolute objector of the Bible, but was notoriously ignorant of its contents. Dr. Johnson, in conversation with several literary friends, once observed, in his usual, direct, and unequivocal manner, that no honest man could be a deist, because no man could be so after a fair examination of the truths of Christianity. When the name of Hume was mentioned to him as an exception to his remark, he replied: 'No, sir: Hume once owned to a clergyman in the bishopric of Durham, that he had never read even the New Testament with attention.'"*

Let us cross-question another important witness as to his knowledge of the book against which he offers testimony. We ask Thomas Paine as to his familiarity with the Bible, which he so bitterly condemns, and he replies, "I keep no Bible." I hold in my hand a sermon preached in New

---

* From " What Noted Men Think of the Bible."

York City, by Rev. W. F. Hatfield, in reply to Mr. Ingersoll's lecture on Thomas Paine, in which reply, with abundant facts, such as would convince a court, it is shown conclusively that Thomas Paine was vicious and corrupt in life, and miserable and remorseful in death. As to the value of Voltaire's testimony against Christianity, Carlyle declares it worthless on the ground of lack of knowledge on the subject of which he testifies. He says: "It is a serious ground of offense against Voltaire that he intermeddled in religion without being himself, in any measure, religious; that, in a word, he ardently, and with long-continued effort, warred against Christianity, without understanding, beyond the mere superfices, what Christianity was."

There are also a class of specialists who are quoted against the Bible, and who manifest a hostility to it, whose testimony is of little value because of the narrow range in which they have studied, making them authorities only in their special department. Halley, the astronomer, once avowed his skepticism in presence of Sir Isaac Newton. The venerable man replied: "Sir, you have never studied these subjects and I have. Do not disgrace yourself as a philosopher by presuming to judge on questions you have never examined."

Distributed Ignorance and Concentrated Hatred—Probable Cause of Ingersoll's Infidelity.

The largest proportion of skeptics, however, are mere sophomores, spoiled with a little learning which is only "distributed ignorance," well represented by a precocious boy of fourteen, whom I found writing an essay on "Matrimony," and who left it during my call to argue in favor of Ingersollism and against the Bible (of which he knew as little as of matrimony), which he admitted he had never read, as do nearly all skeptics when questioned on this matter. The bitterness of the opposition to Christianity of Mr. Ingersoll and other infidels is explained by the Earl of Rochester, who was converted from infidelity and said, in explanation of his former course and that of others: "A bad heart, a bad heart is the great objection against the Holy Book." "The fool hath said in his *heart*" (not his head) "there is no God." The bad heart is father to the infidel thought. It is like the case of the old woman who broke her looking-glass because it showed the wrinkles creeping into her fading face. Men strive to break the Bible glass that shows the wrinkles and defects of character. The whole appearance and tone and spirit of Mr. Ingersoll in his lectures is suggestive of this heart hatred against the book which he attacks, "kicks," "hates," not with the calmness of logic, but with the bitterness of a heart-hostility. Those infidels who have faithfully examined the Bible have usually been convinced of its truth and converted to Christianity. Among them, such distinguished names as Lord Lyttleton, Gilbert West, Soame Jenyus, Bishop Thompson, and at least a score of notable cases in connection with Mr. Moody's revival meetings in England. "What comparison, let us ask, will the number of celebrated skeptics, even when the best possible showing is made, hold with the distinguished men who have ranked the sacred volume above all others? Remember that your mother's love for the Bible and your own early reverence for it, have the indorsement of the grandest and profoundest minds which have been known and honored among humanity."

The Truth of the Whole Matter.

But salvation is not by belief in a book, or a creed, or a Church, but by belief in the person of Jesus Christ. Mr. Ingersoll skips this hard problem, "What think ye of

Christ?" He hardly refers to this citadel of Christianity half a dozen times in all his lectures, making his attacks chiefly on human outposts and then claiming to have overborne the citadel of Christianity. Even Strauss, Renan, Rousseau, Theodore Parker, Napoleon, and Richter—none of them experimental Christians—unite as a jury in the verdict expressed by Richter in regard to Christ, "He is the purest among the mighty, the mightiest among the pure." We have, then, two facts as a sure anchorage of our Christianity to-day. All scholarly skepticism agrees with Christianity that the Bible is the best of books and that Christ is the best of men. He who thus accepts the Bible and Christ can not logically or consistently stop short of a Christian life, following Christ as his pattern, and walking by the Bible as his rule.

We may differ about creeds, and Church forms, and Bible interpretation, but he who has faith and faithfulness toward the person, Jesus Christ shall be saved. Let us then devoutly utter the creed of Daniel Webster, as inscribed by his own request on his tombstone at Marshfield:

" LORD, I BELIEVE, HELP THOU MINE UNBELIEF. PHILOSOPHICAL ARGUMENT ESPECIALLY THAT DRAWN FROM THE VASTNESS OF THE UNIVERSE IN COMPARISON WITH THE APPARENT INSIGNIFICANCE OF THIS GLOBE, HAS SOMETIMES SHAKEN MY REASON FOR THE FAITH THAT IS IN ME; BUT MY HEART HAS ASSURED ME THAT THE GOSPEL OF JESUS CHRIST MUST BE A DIVINE REALITY. THE SERMON ON THE MOUNT CAN NOT BE A MERELY HUMAN PRODUCTION. THIS BELIEF ENTERS INTO THE VERY DEPTH OF MY CONSCIENCE. THE WHOLE HISTORY OF MAN PROVES IT."

CHAPLAIN M'CABE'S REPLY.

The Famous Chaplain has a Remarkable Dream- He Sees the Great City of Ingersollville—Which Ingersoll and the Infidel Host Enter—And are Shut in for Six Months—Remarkable Condition of Things Outside and Inside—Happiness and Misery—Ingersoll Finally Petitions for a Church and sends for a Lot of Preachers.

I had a dream which was not all a dream. I thought I was on a long journey through a beautiful country, when suddenly I came to a great city with walls fifteen feet high. At the gate stood a sentinel, whose shining armor reflected back the rays of the morning sun. As I was about to salute him and pass into the city, he stopped me and said:

"Do you believe in the Lord Jesus Christ?"

I answered: "Yes, with all my heart."

"Then," said he, "you can not enter here. No man or woman who acknowledges that name can pass in here Stand aside!" said he, "they are coming."

I looked down the road, and saw a vast multitude approaching. It was led by a military officer.

"Who is that?" I asked of the sentinel.

"That," he replied, "is the great Colonel Robert I———, the founder of the City of Ingersollville."

"Who is he?" I ventured to inquire.

"He is a great and mighty warrior, who fought in many bloody battles for the Union during the great war."

I felt ashamed of my ignorance of history, and stood silently watching the procession. I had heard of a Colonel

I———, * * * * * * but, of course, this could not be the man.

The procession came near enough for me to recognize some of the faces. I noted two infidel editors of national celebrity, followed by great wagons containing steam presses. There were also five members of Congress.

All the noted infidels and scoffers of the country seemed to be there. Most of them passed in unchallenged by the sentinel, but at last a meek-looking individual with a white necktie approached, and he was stopped. I saw at a glance it was a well-known "liberal" preacher of New York.

"Do you believe in the Lord Jesus?" said the sentinel.

"Not much!" said the doctor.

Everybody laughed, and he was allowed to pass in.

There were artists there, with glorious pictures; singers, with ravishing voices; tragedians and comedians, whose names have a world-wide fame.

Then came another division of the infidel host—saloon-keepers by thousands, proprietors of gambling hells, brothels, and theatres.

Still another division swept by: burglars, thieves, thugs, incendiaries, highwaymen, murderers—all—all marching in. My vision grew keener. I beheld, and lo! Satan himself brought up the rear.

High afloat above the mass was a banner on which was inscribed: "What has Christianity done for the country?" and another on which was inscribed: "Down with the churches! Away with Christianity—it interferes with our happiness!" And then came a murmur of voices, that grew louder and louder until a shout went up like the roar of Niagara: "Away with Him! Crucify Him, crucify Him!" I felt no desire now to enter Ingersollville.

As the last of the procession entered, a few men and women, with broad-brimmed hats and plain bonnets, made their appearance, and wanted to go in as missionaries, but they were turned rudely away. A zealous young Methodist exhorter, with a Bible under his arm, asked permission to enter, but the sentinel swore at him awfully. Then I thought I saw Brother Moody applying for admission, but he was refused. I could not help smiling to hear Moody say, as he turned sadly away:

"Well! they let me live and work in Chicago; it is very strange they won't let me into Ingersollville."

The sentinel went inside the gate and shut it with a bang; and I thought, as soon as it was closed, a mighty angel came down with a great iron bar, and barred the gate on the outside, and wrote upon it in letters of fire, "Doomed to live together six months." Then he went away, and all was silent, except the noise of the revelry and shouting that came from within the city walls.

I went away, and as I journeyed through the land I could not believe my eyes. Peace and plenty smiled everywhere. The jails were all empty, the penitentiaries were without occupants. The police of great cities were idle. Judges sat in court-rooms with nothing to do. Business was brisk. Many great buildings, formerly crowded with criminals, were turned into manufacturing establishments. Just about this time the President of the United States called for a Day of Thanksgiving. I attended services in a Presbyterian Church. The preacher dwelt upon the changed condition of affairs. As he went on, and depicted the great prosperity that had come to the country, and gave reasons for devout thanksgiving, I saw one old deacon clap his handkerchief over his mouth to keep from shouting right out. An ancient spinster, who never did like the "noisy" Methodists—a regular old blue-stocking Presbyterian—couldn't hold in. She expressed the thought of every heart by shouting with all her might, "Glory to God for Ingersollville!" A young theological student lifted up his hand and devoutly added, "*Esto perpetua.*" Everybody smiled. The country was almost delirious with joy. Great processions of children swept along the highways, singing,

> "We'll not give up the Bible,
> God's blessed Word of Truth."

Vast assemblies of reformed inebriates, with their wives and children, gathered in the open air. No building would hold them. I thought I was in one meeting where Bishop Simpson made an address, and as he closed it a mighty shout went up till the earth rang again. O, it was wonderful! and then we all stood up and sang with tears of joy,

> "All hail the power of Jesus' name!
> Let angels prostrate fall;
> Bring forth the royal diadem,
> And crown him Lord of all."

The six months had well-nigh gone. I made my way back again to the gate of Ingersollville. A dreadful silence reigned over the city, broken only by the sharp crack of a revolver now and then. I saw a man trying to get in at the gate, and I said to him, "My friend, where are you from?"

"I live in Chicago," said he, "and they've taxed us to death there; and I've heard of this city, and I want to go in to buy some real estate in this new and growing place."

He failed utterly to remove the bar, but by some means he got a ladder about twelve feet long, and with its aid, he climbed up upon the wall. With an eye to business, he shouted to the first person he saw:

"Hallo, there!—what's the price of real estate in Ingersollville?"

"Nothing!" shouted a voice; "you can have all you want if you'll just take it and pay the taxes."

"What made your taxes so high?" said the Chicago man. I noted the answer carefully; I shall never forget it.

"We've had to build forty new jails and fourteen penitentiaries—a lunatic asylum and an orphan asylum in every ward; we've had to disband the public schools, and it takes all the city revenue to keep up the police force."

"Where's my old friend, I——?" said the Chicago man.

"O, he is going about to-day with a subscription paper to build a church. They have gotten up a petition to send out for a lot of preachers to come and hold revival services. If we can only get them over the wall, we hope there's a future for Ingersollville yet."

The six months ended. Instead of opening the door, however, a tunnel was dug under the wall big enough for one person to crawl through at a time. First came two bankrupt editors, followed by Colonel I—— himself; and then the whole population crawled through. Then I thought, somehow, great crowds of Christians surrounded the city. There was Moody, and Hammond, and Earle, and hundreds of Methodist preachers and exhorters, and they struck up, singing together,

"Come, ye sinners, poor and needy."

A needier crowd never was seen on earth before.

I conversed with some of the inhabitants of the abandoned city, and asked a few of them this question:

"Do you believe in Hell?"

I can not record the answers; they were terribly orthodox.

One old man said, "I've been there on probation for six months, and I don't want to join."

I knew by that he was an old Methodist backslider. The sequel of it all was a great revival, that gathered in a mighty harvest from the ruined City of Ingersollville.

Arthur Frazey

[Photographed by Mosher.]

DR. SWAZEY'S REPLY.

Momentary View of Col. Ingersoll Through the Doctor's Glass— The Bible on the Meridian—What the Doctor Sees in the Great Book.

The genial, eloquent, sensational, unfair, evasive Colonel Ingersoll has come and gone. Nobody has been alarmed. But out of 400,000 people a large audience was found to laugh with him at Moses and the Bible. He eschewed argument altogether. He did not attempt to instruct anybody. He had only a campaign speech to make against— God. This article is simply an invitation to any fairminded doubter to consider the reasonableness of a laugh at the Christian's Bible. Is this book a bad book, or a silly book, just fit for jeer and sarcasm? Take a common-sense view. In order to do so, it is necessary to take a common-place view, to bring to the foreground that which all assailants like to leave in the background, namely, that the Bible teaches by commandment and precept only that which is pure and good.

Relating to man's duty to himself, it teaches personal purity, sexual and otherwise; temperance in meats, drinks, opinions and ambition, responsibleness for inclinations, thoughts and actions; a paramount love for the truth; courage and hopefulness in all lawful purposes; self-improvement, and a cheerful enjoyment of the good things of life. Relating to man's duty to others, the Bible teaches honesty between man and man; restitution when wrong has been done, wittingly or unwittingly; the damnableness of adultery, seduction, and everything that violates the purity of a family or a person; the forgiveness of injuries; a charitable view of human actions, including patience and forbearance, mercy; the duty of life-long usefulness, kindness and helpfulness; a genial temper in social and business life; obedience to magistrates; and a multitude of minor virtues. Relating to the moral order of things, the Bible teaches that wrong-doing is unavoidably the way of sorrow, and right-doing the way of happiness.

These teachings, given not in bald outline, but in fresh and animated pictures and discourses, make up the ethical system of the Bible from the first lesson of the antediluvian age to the last words of the book, which are against whoremongers, and all makers and lovers of a lie, and in praise of all who are just and good. And, still further, in no instance is there left on record an immoral precept, or one which impurity, or injustice, or dishonesty, or unkindness, or selfishness in any form are proposed. There is no mistake in that direction. Still further, we challenge any assailant to name a virtue, acknowledged to be such by the mass of mankind, which is wanting in the catalogue of Bible virtues. The ethical system is as complete as it is pure, as comprehensive as it is sound and true, absolutely covering the whole area of man's duty to himself and to his fellow-man; a system sounding all depths, touching the most delicate fibres of life, and without a flaw or an omission. Its precepts and laws come in their own order, but they all appear in the record first or last. The Buddhistic "decalogue" seems to have been in advance of the Mosaic in this—that it had two commandments wanting in the latter—"Thou shalt not lie," "Thou shalt not get drunk." But these commandments, although not in our own decalogue, are written over and over again in the Old Testament as well as the New. And yet once more the moral requirements of the Bible, are as clear of puerilities as they are of impurity or oblique vision. The Buddhistic decalogue steps right down to a moral weakness of which the Bible is never guilty. "Thou shalt not visit dances nor theatrical representations." "Thou shalt not use ornaments nor perfumery in dress."

Occultation of Ingersoll's Good Sense—General Survey of Deities—Scope of Divine Revelation.

Now the common-sense question occurs whether a book containing such a system, always teaching men what is good and pure, always warning him against evil, and encouraging him to be a strong, sound, pure, complete man in everything, is worthy of sneers, ribaldry and irreverence, even though it were full of unbelievable fables and fantastic ideas of immortality. In what spirit can a company of people shout their applause when a book whose lines of thought are always leading a man above himself is made the target of sarcasm and ridicule, and the cry is almost in so many words, "Down with the Bible!" Let us go a little beyond the strictly ethical. The general ideas of our Bible about God commend themselves to the best wisdom of mankind. We make no reference now to any sect of theologies, but to the theological atmosphere both of the Old and New Testaments, namely, that God is, and being the Creator, the life and force of all things, in other words, as our Bible has it, the Living God, superintends all human affairs. As a Creator He has not forgotten His work; as a Father He is always mindful of His offsprings; and caring for man is leading him on by a great hope to a great inheritance; that His face is against evil doing, that He smiles on all who strive to be just and good, and that in sorrow and want and temptation He folds to His great heart a righteous and even a repentant man; and as the shuttle goes back and forth, knitting into each other the soiled and blood-stained threads, He is weaving therefrom a garment of light for mankind; that superstition, despotism, slavery and war are only other names for His patience, while man is learning the great lesson. This is the Bible interpretation of the incomprehensible Cause and Spirit of the universe, that He is alive, and the Father and Friend of man now, and will have some more for him after the years have rolled by.

Suppose, now, it be all untrue, is there not something in this dream or conceit that should bring a sigh rather than a sneer from the heart of the unbeliever? The god of Brahmanism is an abstraction without attributes, the great nothing of the universe. Much the same is true of Buddhism, only in another way. It has law and virtue, but no God of love, and asks no trust or faith. The same is true in the unchanging round which knows no spirit above and no hope below, taught by Confucius to his disciples. The religion of the Persians presented a god who had a devil-god for a yokefellow, keeping up the eternal and never-to-be-ended quarrel of good and evil. Our Bible begins with the idea that God is one God, the only and the Supreme, and ends with this one God sending angels down to say to the weary world, "Peace on earth good will to men." Away beyond all the faiths and all the Bibles held sacred by mankind, ours alone declares that man is not an orphan, that good and evil are not eternal antagonisms, in other words, that the Great Supreme is our Father in Heaven. True or false, wisdom has taught nothing more inspiring or helpful to man. Neither imagination nor credulity has elsewhere painted a vision so attractive, or out of the "silences" and "eternities," and mysteries, whispered so good a word in the ears of mortals. This idea of lordship and fatherhood is not incidental. It runs through every narration, is implied in every precept, and re-affirmed in every promise. And even if it be beyond proof it makes the whole Bible at least a golden dream.

Suppose now one does not take as absolutely and historically true the story of Adam's rib and the woman, or of the fish swallowing a man and throwing him unhurt on the shore, does not the high moral tone of every command and every precept everywhere illumined by this pure and golden dream, entitle this book to the reverence of mankind? And especially since by the common consent the idea of virtue in our Bible goes beyond the many excellent things of Confucius, Zoroaster and the other sacred writers of other religions, and its idea of the "living God" surpasses in purity and attractiveness, and in consolation and hope, all other religions, is not this purest blossom of the instinct, if you please to call it so, of duty and faith, of inestimable value as the guide and hope of man, even though it were overlaid with ten-fold more difficulties than the most ingenious scoffer can present? Or, if it is not reliable as a guide, is it not worthy of reverence as the proudest achievement of the hungry mind of man?

The Great Central Figure—Absolute Unity of the Bible System.

Still further, this Bible has for its central, or rather terminal, figure a name so remarkable that none but the obscene and profane use it lightly, a man so remarkable that whatever the skeptic may say of Moses or Paul, his tongue would refuse its office should he attempt to catalogue the mistakes of Jesus of Nazareth. Voltaire, Diderot, Bolingbroke, Strauss, Renan, all speak reverently of this One Man of history. And yet the whole New Testament is built up on the sayings and doings of this Man. And not the New Testament only. The Jewish scriptures, full of errors or not, were full of the ideas of a Messiah, from

Moses to Malachi. And this marvelous man claimed that He was that Messiah. So that the Old Testament, as well, is a record of various forms pointing to this Man. I raise here no question of the truth of prophecy; I simply affirm that this Man, whose purity and wisdom are so singularly impressive, claimed to be the fulfillment of those old writings, identified Himself with Moses and David and Isaiah, and sanctified the great current of thought which from the mouths of these men flowed along the shores of that elder world. So that to revile the old Bible of the Jews is to revile Him. There is no scholar, orthodox or liberal, believing or skeptical, who does not identify the phenomenon of Christianity with the phenomenon of Judaism. Out of the soil of Judaic history sprung this purer growth—Jesus and the things He taught.

I suggest, therefore, that before one joins in the laugh against a religion which was founded long anterior to any other historical records than its own, he pause a little, remembering that this remarkable Man, who has not yet become antiquated, quoted those old books as His Bible, and doubtless had a tolerable understanding of their meaning and worth. And, perhaps, if He whose sermon on the mount is yet as fresh in the nineteenth century as though it were uttered to-day, found a vein of precious ore in those books, those same veins may be yet visible in our time.

The Bible Law of Development vs. Infidel Philosophy.

I have given, you will perceive, room for a large amount of the unaccountable and incredible in a Bible worthy of reverence. In fact, there is no occasion, except in the peculiarity of some men's minds, to allow so much. There is a passage in the Bible that is descriptive of the kingdom of Heaven, and reads thus: "First the blade and then the ear, and after that the full corn in the ear." The Bible here gives the key to itself. It is a statement of the law of development, intellectual and moral. An observation of the Bible from the standpoint of this law discovers an answer to the objections that are just now brought against our sacred Book. Col. Ingersoll and men of his style of criticism (and, I am sorry to say, some preachers, also,) quote a verse from Genesis precisely as though the same words, or the same event, were found in the Gospels. They judge an act or a usage recorded in the Pentateuch precisely as though it were found in the Acts of the Apostles. They make no allowance for the stage of human progress. They would teach a child surveying before he had learned the multiplication table. They talk about "skulls" as indicating progress, but God must needs put the same ideas into a skull of the Laurentian period that He does into a skull of to-day. Otherwise, God is worthy of hate. They would preach the doctrine of equality on the deck of a man-of-war. They utterly ignore the drill that men and nations need in coming up to their majority. They would suffer the rabble in a court-room to vote down the decision of a judge on the bench. The men who are historically connected with God's order of things must dispense with the great schoolmaster—experience. Ideas must spring forth complete, like Minerva. Rafters and dome must touch the skies the same day the foundation stones were laid. Those are the ideas with which a certain class of critics approach the Old Testament. If a people are not ripe for a commonwealth, and God gives them a king, God is all wrong. If a people are become a great military camp and Moses proclaims martial law, Moses and his God are monsters of cruelty. If there are no jails, no way of disposing of prisoners of war, and a gentle servitude is the substitute, God is a great slave-driver. If men's lusts are so greedy that even the best of them want more wives than one, the patience of God with the slow growth of moral ideas is translated as the establishment of polygamy. If a people are so vile and filthy that the beasts are clean and modest in comparison, and God sends an army to wipe them out of being, we are pointed to the white faces of women and children lifted on the crests of the divine wrath!

Common Sense View of the Subject—How it Eliminates Polygamy, Slavery, etc.

Common sense, in asking whether the Bible is worthy of confidence would ask whether, as matter of fact, the moral instruction of any period of Bible record was not fully up to the capacity of that period to receive it? It would ask another question—namely, whether a divine tuition is different from any other, except that it is more skillful?—whether, in fact, the critics who compare an old order of things with the highest state of moral development are not demanding that the people under God's training shall be a miraculous people, throwing off prejudices as they do a Winter garment, bearing fruit without any intermediate period of growth and blossom, and, in general terms, upsetting the every day laws of progress. It is this idealism—than which nothing is more irrational—which creates a large share of the moral difficulties of the Old Testament. It is the insane or reckless, the idiotic or perverse tenacity with which men demand that the divine teaching must not suit itself to the time in which it was given, but must always be up to the ripest periods of progress, that gives any opportunity for the objugations of men who "can write a better Bible" themselves than ours.

The two great charges brought against the Bible are polygamy and slavery. Now, admit that in all stages, from the chimpanzee up to Darwin, they are wrong (which is by no means clear), are these charges true? The fact that polygamy and slavery existed among the people who were under drill does not prove it. The fact that there were laws regulating either of these practices does not prove it. A law regulating the social evil does not prove that the sovereign people who make the laws approve the social evil, but only that, if men and women will go wrong, society must put up some defenses against corruption. Common sense inquires whether statutory allowance is an indorsement. And if that Remarkable Man, commenting on the divorce laws of Moses, said that Moses gave those laws because the people could not bear any better laws, common sense inquires if the same may not be true of other recognized usages which are below the ideal of an advanced age.

And when one rails at the Bible for its ill-treatment of women, the railing is simply gratuitous. I have read the Old Testament more or less carefully for many years, but I do not, at this writing, remember a single word that dishonors woman as woman. I have read only a little of Brahminical writings, but I remember a sentence or two about women. "A woman is never fit for independence;" "Women have no business with the text of the Veda. * * * Sinful women must be as foul as falsehood itself. This is fixed law." Whether in the last quotation it is meant that there is no purification for a bad woman, or what else, I do not know; but I do not recall anything like it in the Old Testament. Educated common sense knows that women among the Hebrews occupied a vastly higher level than the women of all other nations. It is simply notorious, that with all the lapses from virtue, the Hebrew women were as white as snow compared with the women of the Gentile world, and honor goes always hand in hand with virtue.

More Common Sense — The Great Ingersoll Orb Approaching the Nihilistic Belt — Nebulæ.

Common sense demands that in judgment of the moral worth of the Bible, it be taken as a whole. The theory of all who receive the Old and New Testaments is that they belong together, are so to be interpreted; that one is the beginning, and the other the conclusion, of the one Bible. The one begins in the " Laurentian period," so to speak, and follows man up from a wild nomad to wealth and empire, and the decay of empire; the moral and the civil law blending and running along together for hundreds of years, then separating by the simple explosion of the civil powers. The other takes him after the wounds caused by the explosion have partly healed, and puts forth moral ideas unencumbered by any considerations of the state. The former gave moral laws to the Jew; the latter moral laws to the man; everything from first to last going on as naturally as the building of a city, or the growth of a tree. And common sense should inquire how it happens, that, while the great army of scholars who have studied these systems, believers and skeptics alike, have been filled with admiration, a man rises up now and then to vituperate the logic of events and malign the great God because He has not chosen to plant a tree with the branches in the ground and the roots in the air.

Common sense naturally asks what the meaning of this bitter outbreak may be. We have no right to men's motives. But this is a phenomenon, the cause of which we have a right to ask, as we would ask the cause of a falling meteor. The Bible is a law and order book. It teaches that one must look out how he pulls up even the tares. Are we in our historic orbit passing a belt of nihilism, a time when assassination is reform, and a bad shot at a poor czar, inheriting semi-barbarism and striving with all his might to get rid of the inheritance, is to be lamented?

You may be told that it is the horrid theology of the Bible which provokes assault. Common sense remarks that, horrid as its theology may be, its sterner features are just like the theology of nature, namely, a demand for obedience to law and "the survival of the fittest." It is nature put into language, the operation of moral causes foretold—that is all. If you want a government more just than one which judges a man according to his deeds, good or bad, and takes into account his knowledge and opportunities, why, the thing to do is to rail at nature, at cause and effect, at seed-time and harvest. For while on the better side the Bible theology is more beneficent than nature, on the hard side it is simply unmitigated natural law. Do the theologians preach that good men will be damned? Then rail at the theologians, and not at the Bible.

In closing this short article, as an addendum, let me ask a question or two for the benefit of all who have a bad opinion of the Bible, as a woman's book or a slave's book.

1. Forget the harem of Solomon, and say why Judaism was a house of refuge for thousands of Roman and Greek women, many of them of noble birth, for a century preceding the Christian era?

2. In the same line, squarely, has, or has not, the modern estate of woman been the fruit of Christian (including Judaic) teaching?

3. Did not the Bible first mitigate and finally destroy slavery in the Roman empire?

4. Did not the Bible destroy slavery in England and America? Charge all the slave-driving you will to Christian men, and give any unbeliever all he claims, and then go down to a last analysis.

5. Are not republican institutions, including (as the old republics did not) democratic ideas, directly and palpably the fruit of the teachings of that remarkable Man (whom the French infidels called the Great Democrat); whose Bible was the Old Testament, and who told His followers how to amend and finish it by a book called the New Testament?

In whatever way these questions may be answered, the man who essays to answer them will find that it is not so easy to eliminate the genius of Moses and Jesus from the genius of the world's movement toward virtue, equality and liberty.

TELL the Prince that this (a costly copy of the Bible) is the secret of England's greatness.—*Queen Victoria.*

I HAVE always said and always will say, that the studious perusal of the Sacred Volume will make better citizens, better fathers and better husbands.—*Thomas Jefferson.*

THE Bible is equally adapted to the wants and infirmities of every human being. No other book ever addressed itself so authoritatively and so pathetically to the judgment and moral sense of mankind.—*Chancellor James Kent.*

CHRIST proved that He was the Son of the Eternal by His disregard of time. All His doctrines signify only, and the same thing, eternity.—*Napoleon Bonaparte.*

I HAVE read the Bible morning, noon and night, and have ever since been the happier and better man for such reading.—*Edward Burke.*

I DO not believe human society, including not merely a few persons in any state, but whole masses of men, ever has attained, or ever can attain, a high state of intelligence, virtue, security, liberty, or happiness without the Holy Scriptures.—*William H. Seward.*

[Photographed by Melander.]

DR. COLLYER'S REPLY.

Dr. Collyer Relates a Little Story—A Book that cost Mr. Ingersoll the Governorship of Illinois—The Volume Philosophically Considered—Heavy Blows.

I have been told a gentleman went to see Mr. Ingersoll once, when he lived in Peoria, and finding a fine copy of Voltaire in his library, said, " Pray, Sir, what did this cost you?" " I believe it cost me the governorship of the State of Illinois," was the swift and pregnant answer. I can not but recall the incident as he stands in the light of his lecture. He seems to be saying, " It is my turn now, and I will do what I can to square the account. I will dethrone your God to-day amid peals of laughter; blow His being down the wind on the wings of my epigrams. I have those about me who will send my words flying all over the state. I will start a crusade which will shut up your churches some day, silence your immemorial prayers, slay all the hopes that would strive after something more than this momentary gleam between the eternities, make of no account the grand deep truth that ' life struck sharp on death makes awful lightning,' and so dwarf our human kind that when we get man where we want him he shall never again be able to look over the low billows of his green graves, and end the fight by making my own creed good once, for all that

   Man, God's last work, who seemed so fair,
    Such splendid purpose in his eyes,
    Who rolled the psalms in wintry skies,
   Who built him fanes for fruitless prayer,

> Who trusted God was love indeed,
>   And love, creation's final law;
>   Though nature red, in tooth and claw,
> With raven, shrieked against his creed;
> Who loved, who suffered countless ills,
>   Who battled for the true and just,
>   *Is* blown about the desert dust,
> And sealed within the iron hills."

Now, since we first knew Mr. Ingersoll by report, there has been a time when those who can only believe in God as a rather helpless little brother, by no means able to take care of Himself, and in themselves as big brothers, who are bound to stand up for Him, might have felt there was grave danger in such a sight as we have witnessed—of a vast array of men and women, some of them it is fair to believe of a thoughtful turn, assembled to hear the last and best word which can be said why God should be dethroned, and His presence and providence numbered among the things that seemed true enough once, but pass away inevitably in the process through which we arise from "our dead selves to higher things."

Sparks Flying in all Directions—Singular Mental Phenomenon Occasioned by $25.000 a Year.

He was clothed once in a fine austerity; went on his lonely way quite content, to give grave and serious reasons for rejecting what so many of us hold dearer than our life, and was faithful to his instinct and insight, though such ovations as were ever given him—as Dr. Dyer used to say of the old abolitionists—might take the form mainly of rotten eggs. I know of more than one man, who, in those days, nourished a deep and most tender regard for him, and found something noble in the stand he made for the best a man can do and be, who has to abide so utterly alone. But Mr. Ingersoll, roystering around as the popular advocate of atheism, at $25,000 a year, as the common report goes, is quite another sort of a man. No doubt the laborer is worthy of his hire. Those who run the thing may be trusted to see to that, and a good many of us who stand on the other side may not be much better, according to the old proverb that it is "money makes the mare go." Still, as this always turns the fine edge of *our* endeavor, and makes us weak for good when we make it at all a matter of barter and sale, so it must be with Mr. Ingersoll, making him weak for what I can not but believe to be evil. He is no more in such a case than the second batch of reformers in the old times, who argued lustily for a reformation, while still they grew rich on the Church lands. No more than your Archbishop, in the Church of England, arguing on the godliness of tythes and priestly authority. So Mr. Ingersoll, in motley, trying to laugh the deepest and most sacred convictions of men down the wind under the guise of girding at the Pentateuch (for we must thank him, I say again, for the frankness with which he tells us this is his ultimate aim), is a very different man to the quiet, manful fellow we used to hear of in Peoria long ago, who won such regard from those who could at all understand him. The man in the ring, whose sole business it is to make you laugh, makes no converts even to rough riding. And so there is ground for neither hope nor fear, as we stand on that side or this, about the advance of atheism, so long as this remains as the best method of its choicest champions. It may make headway with such men as Voltaire had to handle, and in such times; but this serious and deep-hearted race of ours never did take to this kind of thing, and never will. It is only as the crackling of the thorns under a pot.

Nor can this bitter and relentless spirit toward those who differ help the advocates of atheism any more than it does the advocates of the faith. Robert Southey says, in a letter to Sharon Turner, touching the contentions of his time between the sects. "When I hear the dissenters talk about Churchmen, I feel like a very high Churchman myself; but when I hear Churchmen talk about dissenters, I feel that I am a dissenter, too." It was but the bias of a nature, in which the balances were still true, in favor of the side which was dealt with most unfairly. The plea in the mind of one who could look on both sides with a calm concern, that the result of fighting over the lamp should not be to put out the light, or of contending over the nature and properties of the spring to soil the water so that no one could drink at it, be he ever so athirst. Lord Bacon says, "there is a superstition in avoiding superstition, when those think they do best who go farthest; but care should be taken that the good should not be purged away with the bad, which commonly happens when this is the method." So I think it must be with such violent and utter denunciation as this, which lies within the spirit of Mr. Ingersoll's address. It has pleased a very bright and able man in our ranks to fall into accord with him in many things he has to say, and to show how we also hold this ground. I may be old-fashioned, and unfit for a fair judgment, but I am very much of Southey's mind, and when I hear orthodoxy denounced in such a spirit, I say I agree with Mr. Ingersoll nowhere. Here is bigotry of a new shape, denouncing bigots; and I sway to the other side for very charity, and the desire that the most good possible should be found in any evil, and especially that one should think as well as possible of those who can not see as we do, but are still of as fine and clear a grain, and show as noble a soul of self-sacrifice—that uttermost and innermost proof a man can give that he believes he is right.

The Clear Ring of Truth vs. the Dull Thud of the Baser Metal—Potency of Simple Statement—The Doctor's Objections to Ingersoll's Talk.

Now, a man who seeks and loves the truth, must be esteemed in every human society; but so far as my own observation goes, the most of our fights and contentions carried on in such a spirit as this I am trying to touch, end in vast clouds of dust and smoke, in which the clear, shining sun of the truth turns blood-red to our human vision. And those who, even with the best intentions, are forever going about, as we say, with a chip on their shoulder, are likely in the end to be voted a common nuisance. The truth must be told, no matter who gets hurt; the truth, or even semblance of the truth, which smites the man who tells it, and moves his heart so that he has to cry "Woe is me if I preach not this Gospel!" But the truth still comes to us through clear and simple statements which tell their own story, rather than through denial, denunciation, satire, slang, and appeals to the top-gallery. So Channing thought, and the result is, that his best sermons are simply statements of the truth as it had come home to his own heart and mind. So Parker thought, and reading his life again, just now, I find there is nothing the man longed for so much as that he might be quiet, and just let the truth dome itself in his great fine heart and brain, while he regrets bitterly the evil times that compelled him to take to other methods: and the best work he ever did for the deep, still truth, are statements. So John Wesley thought, when once he struck his shining path from earth to heaven, and his sermons from 1740 to 1780, are simply statements of the ever-growing and ever-brightening truth God is revealing to man. And so even Calvin thought, and his earliest and best utterances are still statements, grim, hard, iron-clinched, but all the same the stern and inexorable affirmation, made good for all time, that neither priest nor Pope can play fast and loose with the Most High God. Always you find the greatest and best men when they themselves are at their best making statements, exactly as Jesus does in the sermon on the mount. Saying what is in them simply and sincerely, feeling sure, as Coleridge says, that "no authority can ever prevail in opposition to the truth." So Columbus holds himself before the Council of Salamanca, when a new world is in debate. So Stephenson holds himself before the House of Lords, when he has to answer for his locomotive. So Newton affirms his discovery of the law of gravitation; and Harvey, that of the circulation of the blood. That is the law of all truth-telling in its noblest and best shape, and then the contention, if there is one, is simply the hiss, as Stebbins, of California, said once, when he was speaking in defence of the Chinese, "is simply the hiss the white-hot truth makes when it strikes the black waters of hell."

Here, then, is my radical objection to Mr. Ingersoll's talk, apart from his final aim. It is conceived and done in a narrow and most bigoted spirit, by one who claims, above all things in the world, to be free from bigotry. The men of whom he speaks so unworthily are, take them by and large, worthy men. The things in the five books of Moses, so called, on which the fathers based their creeds, are rapidly passing into worthier meanings; and the day is not far distant when the old belief will have rotted down, and be as when an old tree rots, to become the nursing mother of a bed of violets. No man believes in such things any more, who has read and thought to any purpose; and the man who has not done this, had far better believe in the six days' work and one day's rest, rib, serpent, fall, flood, ark, manna, and all the rest of those wonders, than in Mr. Ingersoll's enormous and most fatal negation of God.

Putting the Fine Edge on Orthodoxy—Taking a Weld with Prof. Swing and Dr. Thomas—Borax and Bigotry.

Nor is that bad and bitter spirit in orthodoxy now which once found utterance in fire and the axe, as it did in far more ruthless ways in atheism when the goddess of Reason was the divinity of France. Orthodoxy, in a free-spoken land like ours, is very civil, indeed, and timid, as I think, almost to a fault, showing just the spirit which is not sure the ground may not slip from under it any moment; and so far as its finest leaders go edging away from the rocking base, as fast and as far the people for whom those men have to care will follow. Nothing could be more gentle than the way orthodoxy used Brother Swing. He was no more orthodox than you are. He might not think so, but that's the truth, patent to the whole world. Yet the church to which he was preaching, and the old standbys, as we call them, said, "This is what we are here for, and have laid out our money and time for, and, if you go back far enough, it is what our fathers shed their blood for. Dr. Swing must be true to his ancient vows, or leave." If Mr. Ingersoll should ever lay out his money, and those of his mind put theirs to it, to build a great hall in Washington or Chicago for the propagation of atheism, and employ a man to preach to them, and then if this man should depart as far backward from their way of thinking as Brother Swing departed forward from that of the Presbyterians, they will be much more catholic and inclusive than I think they are if they use that man as gently.

I do not mention this for proof of my word that orthodoxy is getting to be very civil—indeed, gentle, timid, and even wanting in a proper courage to take care of its own household, if we are to judge from the half-and-half measures they are taking with Mr. Talmadge, in Brooklyn, and the way in which they let him smite them on the mouth.

Orthodoxy has exchanged the old fetters of iron for silken bands with an elastic base. Brother Thomas, my dear and good friend, has no right to preach in a Methodist pulpit, and in the days I remember, would not have preached in one to this time. There must be a certain concert of opinion, capable of being brought within fair lines, or nobody would organize or hold anything. This is the secret of our most happy relation through all these years in this church. We hold together through a large, free, common opinion about certain grand verities. I should injure my own nature if I went over those lines. Yet men are continually going over them in the orthodox churches. But they bear and forbear, scold a little, fret a good deal, and trust the brother may see things different presently or depart in peace, and then, when there is no help for it, they lift him very gently out of the fold.

Nor is the scorn Mr. Ingersoll pours out on these ancient books befitting any man who could feel his way to their heart, apart from any theory of inspiration or the use made of them to hinder human progress. It is the spirit of the Caliph he shows, who, when the question came up what should be done with a superb library, said, "Burn it; whatever is against the Koran ought to be burnt, and whatever agrees with the Koran is not needed." With some such narrow vision he would judge these venerable monuments of the most ancient time; make an end of them to human credence; get them branded for worthless in the interests of human reason; and order himself toward them as if an iconoclast, looking over the treasures of the Louvre, should note only what is grotesque or painful, while he missed what is most beautiful and entrancing, tumble the whole into a heap, and burn it into ashes and lime. Men have misused these books, there can be no doubt of that, and turned some parts of them into bane, which, well used, might bring blessing. So they tell me, there is no place that can match Peoria in its power to turn good grain into whisky; therefore, shovel Peoria into the river, and leave the smiling prairies where the grain grows, a waste.

Nothing in the world shows a man's limitations so fatally as the play of this power which can not or will not distinguish between the use and the abuse of things, or will overlook the abiding good because of the transient evil. We tolerate it easily in the child who turns in wrath on the chair against which he has bruised himself; we look twice at the man who does this, and then draw our own conclusion. I have been told, on good authority, that Mr. Ingersoll, in his childhood and his early youth, did get badly bruised against these books. Well, the books have to take it now; but is this the sign of a large and a gracious mind? One would think he might have gotten over it before this, and come to understand them better than mere instruments of hurt. I can agree in nothing touching the Bible and the soul's life with the man who tells me his aim is to damage or destroy the faith of man in God, to the best of his ability; but if this was out of the way, one might not object to his antagonism to the misuse of Moses by those who think they do God service. Still, in any case, I find too much beauty in the books to allow me to touch them with irreverent hands. They are simply above all standards of value, with which I measure other books outside the Scriptures, in the revelation they make to me of the way men felt their way toward a sure faith in God in those old times, and so grew, in many instances, to be very noble and good at last, and, as I have said, of the way in which they tried to account for this wonderful and mysterious universe in which they found themselves when they had "learned the use of I and me, and said 'I am not what I see, and other than the things I touch.'" Nor would I lose one of the wonders. They all tell us something we want to know about the working of the human mind.

That is a very poor and rude matter I treasure in my study; a broken vase of gray clay, with a few fishbone marks on it; but if there was not another of them in the world I would not exchange it for the Portland vase, for this reason: That on a day, so remote I can not strike it, some poor savage made that vase in my little town, to hold the dust of some one dear to him, put those marks on it for a token of what was in his mind, and then made a little vault and hid it away until the sun of this century should shine on it, and when I hold that vase, I find a trace of the man who had else been lost. There is the faint beat of a human heart lingering in the clay, and a dim remembrance of tears, and the marks, and as if they should open my grave two thousand years from now, and find the white cross still fresh on my coffin, and say, "Tender, loving hands laid that there, let us deal with it tenderly." These rude and half-shapen things in the old books are the clue to the man who made them, and how he felt, and what he thought. I would not spare the least letter out of them, but would scan them in all reverence, let who will scorn them. They all belong to our human history, and it is only their misfortune they have ever been misused. They are included in the saying of the great and wise German, that the Bible begins nobly with Paradise, the symbol of Faith, and concludes with the eternal kingdom; and with the grand, sweet word of Thomas Carlyle: "In the poorest cottage there is one book wherein, for thousands of years, the spirit of man has found light and nourishment, and an interpreting response to whatever is deepest in him. The Book wherein to this day the eye that will look well, the mystery of existence reflects itself, and if not to the satisfying of the outward sense, yet to the opening of the inward sense, which is the far grander result."

A Touching Illustration—Eloquence and Truth—Havelock's Saints.

Of the doctrine advanced by Mr. Ingersoll, and his purpose to have done with the God Jesus believed in, and show reason why we should have done with Him, there is nothing to say if I have not said it steadily these many years. A remark of Charles Hare strikes me forcibly as I read the few words that are said on this matter, in the address, "There is no being eloquent for atheism. In that exhausted receiver the mind can not use its wings—the clearest proof that it is out of its element." For when I consider how eloquent Mr. Ingersoll has been at times, and the moving cause of it, I can see that he also must answer to this law. He never said grander words than those about our boys, their mighty heart, and utter self-sacrifice, for the noblest ends. But there never was anything done since the world stood, in which the presence of God could be traced, and his power felt more clearly, nor did ever men make such sacrifice with a devouter sense that God was within it all, than those most worthy his grand and touching eulogium. "Call out Havelock's saints," Sir Archibald Campbell shouted, when hope was almost dead in the great Sepoy rebellion in India. Something must be done, and done on the swift instant, or there would be more woful work among the women and children. Call out Havelock's saints, *they* are sure to be ready, and they are never drunk. They were of the sort that carry a Bible in their knapsack, and turn to chapter and verse, and sing psalms from old Rouse's version to Dundee and Elgin, and the Martyrs, and nourish their hearts on stories of the way stout battles were fought and grand martyrdoms endured for God among the moors. Call out Havelock's saints, they are always ready, and never get drunk, and they do fight like the very angels. They were but the brothers of the great, simple souls who fought at Ball's Bluff, and in scores of battles beside, while mothers and sisters did the praying for the moment, for they had no time except just to look up and hear that voice in the heart say, "Steady, my boy, steady, you are of a grand stock, you must tell a grand story. And they told it, and at the heart of it all was God. and a new life for the nation, and in time a new civilization that shall shed its blessing on the whole waiting world.

Atheism—Not an Institution but a "Destitution!"—The True Life.

I have no stones to throw at atheism any more than I have stones to throw at blindness. It can never be more than a very sore and sad limitation, not an institution, but a destitution. This Anglo-Saxon nature is not good soil for it; no arguments can make it take hold and grow in us any more than arguments can make roses take hold and grow on Aberdeen granite. Nor have I any exhortation save this: That as we stand as pioneers of the noblest and fairest faith we can reach, a faith which throws no strands to stay itself on the fall, or the flood, or the manna, or the sun, standing still, or any of these old wonders, but just fronts the light and drinks it in, we shall grow ever more worthy to prove God's presence in the world, by revealing it in our life, and in the work he has given us to do. There is no argument like that which lies within a sweet and true life which looks to God forever for its inspiration and its joy. Let us be right worthy of our faith.

>Then shall this Western Goth,
>So fiercely practical, so keen of eye,
>Find out some day that nothing pays but God.
>Served whether in the smoke of battle field,
>In work obscure done honestly—or vote
>For truth unpopular—or faith maintained,
>To ruinous convictions—or good deeds,
>Wrought for good's sake, heedless of heaven or hell.

FRED. PERRY POWERS' REPLY.

The Sinaitic Code—Solvent Powers of the Historic Method—Graphic Illustration of the Two Schools.

CHRISTIANITY, like a fortress on an open plain, is liable to attack from opposite directions. But it is well for the attacking parties to remember that columns of argument do not, like columns of soldiers, co-operate when moving in opposite directions. Christianity is not to be disposed of by proving that at the same time it is and is not a certain thing.

The "historic method," like every new journal, seems "to meet a long-felt want." It has been clutched greedily and employed in every conceivable shape. It proves not only that whatever is is right, but that whatever was was right, and whatever will be will be right. It has been carried to a point where it undermines personal responsibility, and with it Mr. Herbert Spencer, in the conclusion of his Sociology, enjoins the reformer and the philanthropist from activity. It eliminates ethical considerations from the mind of the historian. It closes the eyes of society to the vices of its members, and it lays its hand upon the mouth of the judge before whom stands a man who, as the result of antecedents, and in the natural effort to harmonize himself with his environment, has committed murder.

Now, it is a little singular that this invaluable historic method should be a legitimate weapon against the church, but an illegitimate weapon for the church. If the church is to be allowed to use this weapon freely it will have no difficulty in making a perfect defense for itself, its predecessor and all of its members, no matter how wild or wicked. The historic method is a solvent in which the inquisition disappears, and which at once removes those spots on the robe of religious history, the wars and massacres of the Israelites. I have no disposition to make any such extensive use of the historic method as this. But all matters of history are to be studied as historical, not as contemporaneous. And it is in the last degree uncandid for the opponents of Christianity to make the extremest use of the historic method when it suits their purpose, and then, in dealing with religious history, eliminate ordinary historic perspective. In this latter particular the enemies of the church are not alone. The Reformation brought in a revival of Judaism, and a large section of Protestant Christianity resolutely closes its eyes to the fact that the Mosaic dispensation was given several thousand years ago, and to a race wholly different in its position from any now existing.

The Mosaic dispensation is not the only thing treated in this way. The directions given by St. Paul to a particular church at a particular date are constantly appealed to in the churches as universal law, applicable to all churches and throughout all ages. If a picture with a man in the foreground and an elephant in the background were shown to two savages, one of whom knew something about elephants, and the other of whom did not, the former would insist upon it that the artist was a ignoramus for painting an elephant smaller than a man, and the other would conclude that man was a larger animal than an elephant, because he appeared so in the picture. The former represents a school of atheists who attack the ethics of the Sinaitic code, and the latter represents a school of devout believers who, receiving the Sinaitic code as a matter of revelation, feel compelled to defend it as the truth and nothing but the truth, and the truth for all times and all places. It is worth while to remember at the very outset what both parties to the war waged over the ethics of the Pentateuch seem disposed to ignore, that what are now denounced as the errors of the Sinaitic code were pointed out more than eighteen hundred years ago by the highest authority recognized by the Christian world.

In the Sermon on the Mount Jesus Christ used the following language:

Ye have heard that it hath been said, an eye for an eye, and a tooth for a tooth. But I say unto you, That ye resist not evil; but whosoever shall smite thee on thy right cheek, turn to him the other, also.—Matt. v., 38, 39.

The *lex talionis,* here repudiated, was not a rabbinical interpolation; it was an integral maxim of the Sinaitic code, as the following words, coming shortly after the Decalogue, show:

And if any mischief follows, then thou shalt give life for life, eye for eye, tooth for tooth, hand for hand, foot for foot, burning for burning, wound for wound, stripe for stripe.—Exodus xxi., 23-25.

Free divorce was another Sinaitic error, so called, and in pointing it out Christ gave us the key to the whole Mosaic dispensation, as the following passage shows:

The Pharisees also came unto Him, tempting Him, and saying unto Him, Is it lawful for a man to put away his wife for every cause? And He answered and said unto them, Have ye not read that He which made them at the beginning made them male and female, and said, for this cause shall a man leave father and mother and shall cleave to his wife, and they twain shall be one flesh? Wherefore they are no more twain, but one flesh. What, therefore, God hath joined together, let no man put asunder. They say unto Him, Why did Moses then command to give a writing of divorcement, and to put her away? He saith unto them, Moses, because of the hardness of your hearts, suffered you to put away your wives; but from the beginning it was not so. And I say unto you, Whosoever shall put away his wife, except it be for fornication, and shall marry another, committeth adultery; and whoso marrieth her which he put away doth commit adultery.—Matt. xix., 8-9.

Divine Adjustment of the Moral Law — Progressive Elimination of Polygamy, Slavery, Etc. — Mount Sinai and Mount Calvary.

The "hardness of heart" referred to is evidently the dullness of the intellectual and moral sense that characterized the almost savage slaves of the Egyptians when they came up out of Egypt. Instead of imposing on them an ethical system perfectly complete and perfectly unintelligible to them in their degraded condition, Moses, under direction of divine wisdom, gave them a moral law which they could understand, and which would develop in them a capacity for something purer and higher.

Polygamy was tolerated, not because it was the ideal system; not because the deity of the Hebrews could devise no other, but because polygamy is the natural intermediate station between promiscuity and monogamy. God chose to make a civilized people out of the Jews, not by His creative fiat, but by operating through natural laws of sociology. In due time, when men were prepared for it, the law of permanent and monogamous marriage was promulgated, but it was in advance of public sentiment, as is shown by the fact that when Christ, in the passage above quoted, forbade free divorce, and proclaimed the sanctity of the marital relation, the disciples suggested that if that was the law it was better not to marry.

So slavery was tolerated under the Mosaic law. But servitude for a short term of years was substituted for permanent and hereditary servitude, and the law threw some protection about the person of the slave. The Mosaic dispensation is not responsible for a defense of slavery. It tolerated an intermediate state between barbarism and civilization.

A fact of vast importance to notice is that this Mosaic system contained within itself the seeds which, when humanity had outgrown the old dispensation, would mature into a new dispensation so far in advance of human attainments, that after nearly nineteen centuries the human race has not begun to catch upon it. Christ expounded the Old Testament references to Himself, beginning with Moses. When Sinai had reduced society to order, and stamped out paganism, then Calvary came and appealed to all that was highest and purest in man. Even at this late day there are not many souls that really comprehend the full meaning of Calvary and whose lives give evidence of that fact. When any considerable portion of the human race has received all that Calvary can confer, a new dispensation may be expected.

In this sense the Mosaic dispensation was perfect and complete. As promulgated on Mount Sinai, it was adapted only to a certain low condition of mankind. But it contained a vital principle, which enabled it to expand as fast as civilization advanced. Starting with the Decalogue, it developed the penitential psalms and the noble exhortations of the prophets, and finally the Beatitudes. Beginning with a catalogue of penalties, it in course of time developed sorrow for sin, and at last that love to God which withholds from sin. This system of religion has developed faster than civilization has advanced. The Israelites at the foot of Mount Sinai probably knew something of the wrongfulness of murder, theft and adultery. But, to-day, in spite of great moral advances—to-day, nineteen centuries after Christ—how much does the human race really know about " hungering and thirsting after righteousness?" Let the foolish declaration that we have outgrown Christianity come from those who have been filled, and who still want something more.

The Decalogue is by no means the complete moral code that it is often represented to be, and it would be singularly out of place in a Christian church were it not that, even to-day, and in the United States, there are many persons incapable of comprehending the Beatitudes which comprehend all there is in the Decalogue, and vastly more. The seventh commandment does not apply to crimes, both participants in which are unmarried, and the Mosaic law treated the seduction of an unbetrothed bondmaid as a trivial offense, sufficiently atoned for by the sacrifice of a ram. The seduction of a free maid, if she was not betrothed, was atoned for by marriage. It was on account of the "hardness of their hearts," their infancy in ethics, that this easy-going statute regarding the sexes was enacted. But Christ said :

Ye have heard that it was said of them of old time, "Thou shalt not commit adultery;" but I say unto you, That whosoever looketh on a woman to lust after her hath committed adultery with her already in his heart.—Matt. v., 27, 28.

The Decalogue said, "Thou shalt not kill," but Jesus Christ added to this as follows :

Whosoever is angry with his brother without a cause shall be in danger of the judgment.—Matt. v., 22.

The Decalogue forbade the bearing of false witness; it was silent as to ordinary mendacity. In the New Testament this law is extended to cover all untruthfulness.

Purpose and Potency of the Mosaic Law.

The purpose of the Mosaic law was to start the Israelites on the path of spiritual enlightenment. It was a provisional system, superseded at the right time by Christianity. The sacrifices were fines imposed on the guilty. They were also daily reminded of the existence of God, and the blood pouring from the altar taught the serious nature and fatal consequences of sin as nothing else would. Of course, to a set of modern sophists, who deny the existence of sin, the sacrifices are simply meaningless, revolving spectacles; but the man who hasn't studied the subject enough to understand the meaning of the Hebrew sacrifices is estopped from discussing them in public.

The barbarities of the Mosaic system form a pet subject of denunciation by gentlemen who have a repugnance to study, coupled with a mania for delivering lectures, when the latter can be done at a pecuniary profit. If a man thinks it just as well to worship the sun or a bull as to worship Jehovah, of course he will regard the penalties denounced against idolatry as tyrannical and barbarous. But no man, unless he has a purpose to accomplish thereby, can shut his eyes to the barrier that idolatry places in the way of mental or moral progress, or both. The interests of the human race demanded that paganism should be roofed out somewhere, if not everywhere. The promise to Abraham, that in his seed should all the nations of the earth be blessed, has been fulfilled, but that has been accomplished only by the most rigorous hostility to paganism among the Jews. In spite of all the stern laws of Moses, Israel again and again relapsed into paganism; yet it was an absolute necessity that if what we now know as civilization was ever to come, paganism must in some corner of the world be stamped out, and the way prepared for Christianity. To teach the Israelites what a moral contagion was idolatry, they had to be taught that it was a physical contagion, contaminating everything connected with the idolator. Had not this been done, the Israelites would have remained, like all the rest of the world, immersed in the unspeakably unclean worship of Baal and Astarte and Moloch. Cost what it might, the ravages of the pestilence had to be checked somewhere.

Excessive Wickedness and Proportionate Punishment—The Court of Heaven vs. the Court of Earth.

Of course, the wars of the Israelites and the annihilation of certain tribes are held to be horrible cruelties by the sophists of the present day. But we are distinctly told that it was for their extraordinary wickedness that these tribes were exterminated. We are again and again told that it was for the wickedness of the Amalekites that their destruction was commanded. We get some glimpses of the unmentionable vileness of some of these Canaanitish tribes. The fact was that they were ulcers on the body of the human race which had to be cut out. Possibly the innocent suffered with the guilty, and possibly there were no innocent except the infants, whom it would have been no mercy to save after their unclean parents were destroyed. It is probable that the moral taint had so rooted itself in the physical system that, had the children been spared, they would have inevitably developed into adults as unclean as their parents. The passages sometimes quoted to show that Jehovah was vindicative, are passages aimed at sin. The most ample amnesty to the repentant is promised from one end of Genesis to the other end of Revelation. The people who denounce the divine government, as manifest in the Old Testament, either deny that there is any such thing as sin, or, which is often the case, they have admirable reasons for being angry because sin is punished. The gentlemen who denounce the destruction of Sodom are necessarily apologists for the Sodomists.

When malignancy is charged against Jehovah it is important to remember that the presence of five righteous persons would have saved Sodom. There was only one righteous person, and not only was he enabled to escape but he secured immunity for his family. Nineveh was spared because the people repented. The Israelites were delivered from their enemies when they forsook their sins. On the other hand Nathan's rebuke to David is a matter of record, and Solomon's licentiousness was punished by the revolt of Jeroboam and the ten tribes. The statement that Jehovah disregarded distinctions of right and wrong, or treated the innocent and guilty alike, or took pleasure in the death even of the wicked is false, and known to be so by the persons who make it. The very sentiment of humanity which prompts certain persons to denounce the divine government of the Jews is found only where Christianity, the legitimate successor of Judaism, prevails.

What are denounced as massacres committed by the Israelites were judicial executions performed under the orders of the only court in the universe which has perfect information of the cases tried before it, and which is perfectly free from weaknesses. To object to the judgment one must either show that the condemned were innocent, which at this late day can not be shown, or one must show that the crimes were less heinous than the court held them to be, which is to become an apologist for crimes of every character, some of which are not even to be named. It is also to be remembered that the divine government is the creator of society, instead of the creature of society, as is human government. The former is, therefore, not to be judged precisely as the latter is, even though abstract justice is the same in Heaven that it is on earth. The charge of vindictiveness is absolutely without foundation; and, by the way, of all the nations known to the Jews the one we might suppose them most hostile to is the Egyptian, for it was in Egypt that the Israelites were enslaved and maltreated. Yet the divine command, coming from Moses, was that the Israelites should in no case oppress the Egyptians, and the reason was that they were once sojourners in the land of Egypt, the very reason we might suppose why they should be especially bitter toward the Egyptians.

Able Bodied Mendacity and Civilization—Love and Obedience.

There is a good deal of dense ignorance or able-bodied mendacity in circulation regarding the ethics of the New Testament. Jesus Christ and His apostles upheld neither political nor domestic despotism. But it is a fact which lecturers should understand that civil order is the first step toward civilization. Despotism is more conducive to civilization than anarchy is. Furthermore, when Paul wrote his epistles the Roman officials suspected all Christians of being hostile to the government, and it was especially necessary that the Roman power should understand by the loyalty of the Christians that He whom they called their king was a spiritual sovereign, and not a rival of the emperor.

What Paul at a particular time wrote to a particular church is by no means necessarily a universal law. What is particularly to be noted is that the exhortations to obedience on the part of the citizen, the wife, the child and the servant are coupled with and conditioned on exhortations to the ruler, the husband, the parent and the master, which certain uncandid and irrational persons, some of whom are inside the church and some of whom are outside of it, are careful to ignore. In Ephesians v. 22, Paul commands wives to submit themselves to their husbands, but in the twenty-fifth verse husbands are commanded to love their wives as Christ loves His church. Now, if the husband fulfills his part of the mutual obligation, the wife's submission will not be of a very mental character. In Ephesians vi. 1, children are commanded to obey their parents, but in the fourth verse fathers are commanded not to provoke their children to wrath, but to bring them up in the nurture and admonition of the Lord. In the next verse servants are commanded to obey their masters, but in the ninth verse we read, "And, ye masters, do the same things unto them, forbearing threatening, knowing that your Master also is in Heaven; neither is there respect of person with Him." In Hebrews xiii. 17, we read, "Obey them that have the rule over you, and submit yourselves; for they watch for your souls as they that must give account." The command to obey rules is conditioned on the discharge of their duties by the rulers.

Now, in omitting one half of each double command, and on the strength of the other half arraigning Christianity as the ally of domestic and political tyranny, modern "free thought" is accomplishing a great work, is it not? The distinguishing characteristic of "free thought" seems to be that it is thought freed from all subservience to facts.

Mr. Powers' Pungent Peroration.

Theology has made many shipwrecks by an excess of *a priori* reasoning, and by reasoning deductively when the means of reasoning inductively exist. But what is termed materialism is habitually doing the same thing, if it can make a point against Christianity by so doing. The enemies of Calvinism have denounced it because it promoted immorality. Yet a severer code of morals would be difficult to find than that maintained by the English Puritans, the Scotch Covenanters, and the French Huguenots, all Calvinists. Would it not be just as rational to judge Calvinism by its fruits as to judge its fruits by Calvinism?

When man has argued from the New Testament that Christianity must be the ally of despotism, and then looks about him and sees that civil liberty is not known outside of Christian lands, and has its fullest development in England and America, where Christianity in its simplest forms prevail, and where there are the fewest barriers between the human soul and the New Testament itself; when he has argued from the New Testament to show that Christianity is inimical to the best interests of womanhood, and then looks around and sees womanhood honored only in Christian countries, constantly employed by and honored in the church, must it not occur to him with painful force that he is a good deal off the track?

It would not be necessary to remind philosophers of the fact, but it is necessary to remind sophists that the Jews did a good many things that the Mosaic dispensation is not responsible for, and that it is mere idiocy to hold Christianity responsible for everything done by individuals or associations in its name. The man who can not discriminate between the legitimate results of a system, and the abuses grafted on to it by its professed adherents, is plainly unfit to debate philosophical questions.

If people made half the effort to understand the Bible that they make to discard it, they wouldn't be so funny as they are now, but they would know more.

THERE are over two hundred passages in the Old Testament which prophesied about Christ, and every one of them has come true.—*D. L. Moody.*

IN regard to the Great Book, I have only to say it is the best gift which God has given to man. All the good from the Saviour of the World is communicated through this Book. But for this Book we could not know right from wrong. All those things desirable to man are contained in it. I return you my sincere thanks for this very elegant copy of the Great Book of God which you present.—*Abraham Lincoln, on receiving a present of a Bible.*

I DEFY you all, as many as are here, to prepare a tale so simple and so touching, as the tale of the passion and death of Jesus Christ, whose influence will be the same after so many centuries.—*Denis Diderot.*

THE Bible is the best book in the world. It contains more of my little philosophy than all the libraries I have seen.—*John Adams. (Second President of United States.)*

AND, finally, I may state, as the conclusion of the whole matter, that the Bible contains within itself all that, under God, is required to account for and dispose of all forms of infidelity, and to turn to the best and highest uses all that man can learn of nature.—*Chancellor Dawson.*

THE Bible is the only cement of nations, and the only cement that can bind religious hearts together.—*Chevalier Bunsen.*

THE Bible is the Word of God—with all the peculiarities of man, and all the authority of God.—*Prof. Murphy.*

FROM the time that, at my mother's feet, or on my father's knee, I first learned to lisp verses from the sacred writings, they have been my daily study and vigilant contemplation. If there be anything in my style or thoughts to be commended, the credit is due to my kind parents in instilling into my mind an early love of the Scriptures.—*Daniel Webster.*

THE same divine hand which lifted up before the eyes of Daniel and of Isaiah the veil which covered the tableau of the time to come, unveiled before the eyes of the author of Genesis the earliest ages of the creation. And Moses was the prophet of the past, as Daniel and Isaiah and many others were the prophets of the future.—*Prof. Guyot.*

WE are persuaded that there is no book by the perusal of which the mind is so much strengthened and so much enlarged as it is by the perusal of the Bible.—*Dr. Melville.*

[Photographed by Mosher.]

BISHOP CHENEY'S REPLY.

How the Question of Forgery Applies to the Five Books of Moses.

In looking at almost any object in the world of nature round about, it becomes remarkable only from certain points of view. The cathedral rocks that form one of the glories of the Yosemite Valley differ not much from any other great pile of jagged cliffs, except in a certain position, where the great mass of Gothic spires and arches appear clothed with evergreen ivy. Only as you reach a certain point where Profile Notch penetrates the White Mountains, do you see far up, up on the topmost cliff, the formation of a face cut in the solid granite by nature's own chisel. But the case of alleged forgery before us is extraordinary from every point of view, for forgery is generally something which concerns some brief document, something that requires only a signature in order to secure its currency. The longer and more elaborate the document which forgery produces, the more danger there must inevitably be of its final and ultimate detection. But here are five long historic books. They are full of details. They cover vast periods of time. They enter into a variety of topics. Incidentally they discuss not only questions of religion, but of law, of politics, of commerce, even of hygiene—medical laws of health. Was ever forgery committed before or since on such a gigantic scale as this? Moreover, there is no crime that is liable to be so speedily detected as forgery. The man who signs some document with another's name rarely goes down to the grave without meeting his punishment here on earth. Why, only a few weeks ago, the doors of our penitentiary, in the State of

Illinois, closed upon a prisoner who had affixed the name of another, whose name was better than his own, to a check upon which he had received the money; but only one month intervened as a gap between that crime and the punishment it merited and received.

It was a hundred years ago, that Thomas Chatterton, one of the most wonderful men, or boys, I might rather say, that England has ever produced, forged a huge mass of papers, professedly historical, that were dated away back in the thirteenth and fourteenth centuries. The style was that of the monks and chroniclers, which he had imitated with the greatest possible perfection. The references to the customs of that ancient period were such as to avoid detection, and Chatterton, in the precocity of his intellect, and in the versatility of his talent, was without a peer in English literary history. The English literary world received it as a revelation out of lost centuries. The great scholars of England were deceived. But it only took three years to expose to every eye the fraud that had been committed, and Chatterton, whom Wordsworth called the "marvelous boy," ended his career in a suicide's grave. O, brethren! who can count the years, who can enumerate the centuries which have rolled over this world of ours since the alleged forgery of this man Moses! And yet to-day, after the lapse of centuries, there are more people who believe in that forgery as the genuine work of the man whom God appointed the great law-giver and leader of Israel, there are more people who hang their hopes for time and eternity on this alleged fraud, and that which has grown out of this alleged fraud—the Gospel of our Lord Jesus Christ—than ever before in two thousand years. Am I not then justified in saying that if this be a forgery, which is contained in the five books of Moses, it is the most extraordinary forgery that has ever been committed in the world since words expressed human thought, or human beings learned to wield a pen?

The "Common Ground" of the Contending Parties—Logical Position of Ezra.

Now, in the first place, I desire to call your attention to certain facts concerning the Mosaic record. In all controversies in every department of human thought there are certain points which are regarded as neutral ground. When our great civil war shook this land from centre to circumference and two mighty armies were face to face in the Valley of the Tennessee, the stars and stripes floated in the same breeze that wafted the stars and the bars; the strains of "Dixie" and "My Maryland" commingled with "Hail Columbia" and the "Star-Spangled Banner;" the soldiers of the different armies exchanged such commodities as they possessed, as if they had been neighbors in peace at home. No wonder that finally it came to pass that between these armies there was what is known as neutral ground, on which it was agreed that the soldiers of one side should not fire on those of the other. Now, is there any such ground as that between those who defend what are known as the five books of Moses, and those who declare they were never written by Moses at all? Is there any point, I say, in this controversy where the skeptic and the believer can come to stand upon one common ground? If we can find such a neutral ground as that, it will save us a long, tiresome, profitless debate.

Now, such a ground I think we have in the life and history of Ezra, the writer of the book of the Old Testament, which bears his name. It is conceded on all hands that this man was a scribe of the Jewish law after the close of the Babylonian captivity. After the people had returned from the land of their exile into the land of their fathers, he gathered into one great collection all these sacred writings that were held by the Jews to be the inspired word of God. No infidel that I am aware of has ever questioned the fact that in this collection of Ezra was contained the five books of Moses. It has been claimed by some of the least scholarly of infidels that Ezra wrote those five books. But that idea was found visionary and was long ago given up by those who opposed the truth of Christianity. But the fact remains that no one, Christian or unbeliever, to-day questions the historic fact that the five books of Moses, as we now accept them, were received as the writings of the lawgiver of the Jewish people when Ezra was at the acme of his influence after the Baylonian captivity. But they state that it was universally conceded that it was four hundred and fifty years before the birth of Christ. In other words, it was admitted that every Jew who returned out of the Babylonian captivity, held these five books to be the works of Moses, the man of God, twenty-three hundred years ago.

The Bishop Planting Signals on the Mountain Tops of History—Survey of the New Moses Air Line.

We stand, then, without dispute, without any controversy, at this point of time—four hundred and fifty years before the birth of our Lord and Saviour Jesus Christ. Now, fix that point in your memory while I attempt, like a civil engineer penetrating some wilderness, to plant the signal on some more remote mountain top of history. Now, all the ancient writings, whether Egyptian or Chaldean, corroborate the testimony of the Bible that these Hebrews were slaves in the land of Egypt. They also agree that they migrated into Southern Syria, under the leadership of a man who was called Moses—a word which meant "one drawn out of the water." It is also universally allowed that they settled in this new land, which had long before been promised to their fathers, about the year 1450 before Christ. We have established then our second date—a date which no skeptic has ever called in question. When our great tunnel that brings the pure water of Lake Michigan into every home and household in this city was in process of construction, the workmen began at either end. There was a shaft out in yonder crib, and there was another on the shore, and underneath the waves the two parties of toilers worked toward each other. And so it is with us. We tunnel between our two shafts. The date 450 B. C. and the date 1450 B. C.—only one thousand years are to be accounted for. Does that seem a long period of time to you? I admit that it does, but not in the history of nations. It is only a trifle more than the time in which you and I are living is removed from the time of William of Normandy, who conquered Harold and the English barons.

Now we will cross the sea to the old tower that still recalls the memory of William the Conqueror. We will enter the office of public records, and in that fire-proof vault, guarded as they guard the specie that is gathered into the treasury of the nation, is a book in two huge volumes of vellum. It is known as the "Doomsday Book." In the year 1086, eight hundred years ago, remember, William the Conqueror caused that record to be prepared. It is nearly as old as the five books of Moses, the Pentateuch, was in the days of Ezra the scribe. But not a page of the "Doomsday Book" has been lost; not a line has been altered; not a letter erased. Its pages read to-day as they did in this old time when the Norman heel was on the Saxon neck—eight centuries ago. The ink is as fresh on the parchment as though that parchment were unstained by age. Do you ask how it is that the record has remained uncorrupted? Do you ask how it is that after all the revolutions that have swept over England, after all the changes of royal houses, and the dissolutions of powerful parties, that that has remained perfectly unaltered? The answer is a perfectly easy one to give. It is because "Doomsday Book" contains the name of every man, who, in the days of William the Conqueror, owned one rood of English soil. It contains a description of the lands throughout the realm. It gives the boundaries of every great estate, and every old English family must, therefore, find the roots of its genealogy in that old book of the early times of the Norman conquest. It gives the title to every acre of land in England. Thus, two of the strongest motives that can influence the human mind and the human will, have conspired to guard this "Doomsday Book" with a jealous and tireless care.

The possession of a great name, and the possession of landed property are wrapped up in England in the safety of that one book. Now, exactly the same motives conspired for the preservation, from all corruption, of the five books of Moses. They contain the list of those who came out of Egypt with Moses and entered into Palestine; they gave a description of the land that was apportioned to each and every name. To lose these books, which the Jews ever regarded as a precious treasure, the genealogy of their household—to suffer them to be tampered with, was to unsettle the title to every man's field from Dan to Beersheba.

If the "Doomsday Book" has survived, uncorrupted, what reason on earth is there to doubt that the Pentateuch was preserved intact during the thousand years that intervened between the time of Moses and the time of Ezra? But I need not stop here. Ezra, as I have said, was one of the captives who returned out of exile. But Daniel, long before the time of Ezra, speaks of this law of Moses. He bases his own conduct and his own private character upon it. Daniel brings us a hundred years nearer to the days when Moses gave that law to the world. When King Josiah mounted the throne of Judah he found that throne polluted by the wickedness that characterized the reign of his father, King Manasseh, and then there came an overwhelming and powerful revival of religion throughout the kingdom. Monarch and subject united in humiliation before God. Numbers of people bowed down before the Jehovah whom they had offended. But we all distinctly know that the root and the seed out of which this revival sprung was the finding of the copy of the five books of Moses, and learning there what Moses had commanded against the sin of idolatry. I have reached a point nearer yet to the time of Moses himself. I will hasten on.

Termination of the Great Air Line.

One thousand and four years before Christ, Solomon regulated the temple service and worship, but he regulated it, we are distinctly told, according to the law that was contained in the Pentateuch. And we are within four hundred and fifty years of the death of Moses. But David refers constantly to the five books of Moses in the psalms. The law of Moses was the foundation on which all the religious character of the psalms of David rest. Before David was Samuel. His entire career pre-supposes the existence of the Mosaic books. But only three hundred and fifty years intervened between Samuel and Moses. Joshua succeeded Moses as the leader of the chosen people. Again and again in his addresses to the people, did he reprove, exhort and encourage Israel, but everywhere on the basis of the books of the law of Moses. Thus, we have link by link carried back this chain of testimony to the very days in which Moses lived. Now we want no better proof than that in the secular history. Suppose the farewell address of George Washington had been made the object of skeptical criticism; suppose that it had been denied that it had been written by Washington, and if I find it alluded to in Mr. Lincoln's address at the monument-raising in Gettysburg; if I find in one of his speeches that President Polk also spoke of it; if this is true of Mr. Van Buren, and Mr. Madison before him, and if even John Adams, the successor of George Washington in the presidential chair, refers to that address—why then, every sensible man will say that it is the nearest equivalent of mathematical demonstration that can possibly be given of the genuineness of the document to which I have referred.

Genealogical Reflections.

Now, I want you to notice again that if these writings were forged, they were forged by men, who even in so doing, blackened the character of their own lineage and ancestry. It has been well said that a man whose chief glory is in his ancestors, is very like a potato—the best part of him is under ground. But after all there is no good man who does not rejoice—and thank God for the fact—when he is able to trace back a long line of God-fearing, pure-living, honest men and women as the seed from whence he sprang. If I go to work and forge a genealogy for myself, I certainly will not manufacture one that describes my forefathers as the blackest set of criminals that ever escaped from a penitentiary. No one pretends for a moment that any one but the Jews were those who could have been responsible for the Testament records; but it they forged it they must have had some motive. Forgers always have a motive. There is something before their minds that is to be gained. But what did these forgers do? Why they compiled a record of their own family tree, that overwhelmed their fathers with everlasting shame and contempt. They described the ancient Hebrews as besotted idolaters in the land of Egypt. When God promised them a land, all their own, flowing with milk and honey—when all that was set before them—they were willing to give up all hope of prosperity, all hope of deliverance from slavery, if they might only have that which they sighed for—the fish and the leeks and garlic of Egypt. They are represented as bowing down to the worship of a calf, which their own hands had made out of their golden ear-rings, and doing that in the very presence of God, displayed upon Mount Sinai, and are described when they reached the borders of the promised land, when all its glory was before them, and its liberty was almost theirs, as being too cowardly to fight the battles that were necessary to gain the possession of their inheritance, till at last God refused to let one of the miserable, cowardly generation enter the land He had promised to their fathers. Yet all this is forgery, not of the Assyrians, not of the Egyptians, who were their hereditary enemies; not of the Philistines, but themselves—the forgery of the Jews themselves. As though in the dead of night a man should steal out under cover of the darkness to the tombstone of his dead father, and with chisel and mallet in hand try to erase the honorable record of his life, and forge a lying epitaph that made him the vilest scoundrel that ever polluted the earth. Nay, if I commit a forgery on my family record, if ever I try to impose a fabulous family tree on those who know me, I don't think I shall ever trace my line to Cæsar Borgia.

Cutting the Gordian Knot.

Now again I would like to notice very briefly some of the objections to the credibility of the Mosaic writers. Now, there is nothing easier than to start difficulties on any subject which the human mind can give attention to. Let a child in its tiny fingers grasp a pin and

7

get at the silvered side of a mirror, and in five minutes it will do more damage than the most skillful laborer can remedy with the work of many hours.

Is it wonderful that the Bible has been made the subject of repeated attacks? I no more hope to answer all the objections that can be put against a book such as the book in question, or even the books of Moses—I say I can no more hope to answer all these attacks than in this springtime I can hope to pick off every green leaf that starts out upon every spreading tree. It were an easier and more effective way to girdle the tree itself. God girdles the tree of infidelity by revival.

If the record of experience tells any fact in the world, it is this, that a thousand objections which the head can see, vanish into thin air when the spirit of God gets hold of a man's heart. Why, there are men here to-night who remember the hour when they found difficulties upon every page of the word of God, when they objected to every principle it propounded, and now look back to the difficulties they used to find there, and wonder how it was possible that they could ever have been troubled by difficulties so palpably absurd. They did not study out one by one the replies that might have been made to these objections. When, in June, huge swarms of flies make our city like the land of Egypt in the days of old, we never undertake to kill them one by one : half a million of people would not be sufficient for that. But God's west wind blows, and they are scattered. So it is that the winds of God's spirit sweep away the swarms of difficulties that men find in the Bible. And yet I am prepared to-night to take up two or three of the objections which have been urged against the credibility of the Pentateuch. These objections resolve themselves into two different parts—the one to the facts of the history of Moses, the other to the morality of the acts that are there recorded, or the precepts that are there laid down. I won't have time to go over both branches of the subject. The limits of such a sermon as this absolutely forbid it. I speak now of the facts. At some future time I hope to take up the moral portion of it.

Now, every time you visit the South Park, you find a place of rest under the grateful shade of an ancient willow. The vast expanse of its gigantic branches, the immense girth of its trunk are the witnesses of its venerable age. If I should take up to-morrow the report of the park commissioners and find there the statement that they, at vast expense, had transplanted that willow tree from the native soil in which it grew to adorn Chicago's pleasure-ground, I should know beforehand that it was false; the very appearance of the tree gives the lie to the statement, and if there were any way in which I could examine the rings that made up the trunk, I need only count them to have a positive proof of the fact that the statement contained in the report was false.

Now, precisely akin to that is the accusation that is often brought against the Book of Genesis. It is said that Moses declares that six thousand years ago God created this world in which we are living now. But we only need to count the geologic strata—we only need to number the rings of the huge trunk of this earth in order to disprove the statement.

The Bishop's Challenge—Moses and Ingersoll as Chronologists.

Now, in reply to this difficulty, which is so often urged against the Book of Genesis, I want to say one word, and that is, I challenge any man in this congregation—I challenge any man in the wide world that has ever read the Bible, to find in any book of the Bible, much less in the Book of Genesis, the statement that the creation of this earth took place six thousand years ago. This Moses, whom Col. Ingersoll thinks was such a blunderer; whose mistakes have been the subject of his jeers and blasphemous ridicule, was a more careful man than our Peoria skeptic thinks. He certainly was careful not to fix the time at which God created this earth. Whether that creation took place six thousand or six million years ago, he does not state. He does say that "In the beginning God created the heavens and the earth." But that is all. All that he asserts is, that matter—the substance out of which the earth was made—is not eternal: it had a beginning; He did create it.

Well, then, again, the creation of man, equally with that of the world, is made the object of attack. We are told that the Bible claims that between five and six thousand years ago God placed the first pair of the human family in Eden. But when geologists have dug down into the formations that make up this globe—formations which upon mathematical calculation have taken ages and ages to produce — they find there the remains of ancient tools, weapons, ornaments and utensils that prove that man must have lived in a time far ante-distant to that of Adam.

For example, the skeleton of an Indian was exhumed some years ago, while digging for the foundation of the gas-works in the City of New Orleans, and it was alleged by one geologist of that day that it could not have been less than fifty thousand years ago that that man lived. It has been flaunted in our faces that science and religion are opposed to each other; that the Bible is against progress, and that we all must concede that the Pentateuch is but a tissue of falsehood.

Now the first answer I have to give is, that there is not one syllable in the Bible that fixes the length of time or man's existence upon this earth. Not one syllable. Moses does not tell us anything about the date that God created Adam and put him in the garden of Eden. True, we have in the New Testament, in the genealogy of Christ, a statement of the number of generations from Abraham down to the Saviour; but who knows precisely what is the meaning of the term "generations?" The word is used in a variety of senses in the Bible, and it baffles all calculation to determine how many ages intervened between Adam and Abraham. The wisest scholars have been perplexed to fix the number of centuries that rolled over the world in that period of time. To say that God placed man upon this earth six thousand years ago, is not quoting the Bible. I want you to remember that. I want you to tell it to the skeptic that picks out genealogical difficulties in the Scripture. It is only repeating the result of calculations in chronology of certain fallible men who, as fallible, were liable to be mistaken. All infidels do it in trying to fasten upon the Scripture the blunders of mistaken men. But, as is well known, the tendency of the best geologists in our day is rapidly going away from the old ideas of the vast periods of time in the construction of this earth.

Mud Calendars vs. Facts—Some Sad and Sorrowful Scientific Figuring in the Sand.

It was not very long ago that Sir Charles Lyell, the distinguished English geologist, calculated from his own standpoint the rate at which the mud is deposited in the great delta of the Mississippi. By actual figures he reached the astounding calculation that the formation of the delta of the Mississippi must have occupied not less than one hundred thousand years. And, when down underneath that deposit a skeleton was exhumed, it proved beyond all question that not less than fifty thousand years ago human feet had trod the soft soil of the delta of the Mississippi.

But unfortunately for Sir Charles Lyell, American geologists were on his track, and the United States coast survey followed in the pathway where he had been investigating. Gen. Humphrey, of the American army, measured accurately the amount of the deposit. He reviewed the figures of the English geologist, and he showed unanswerably that the whole delta of the Mississippi could not have been in process of formation longer than four thousand four hundred years. For many years geologists held that a quantity of pottery that was found some sixty feet below the surface of the soil, in the delta of the Nile, was at least twelve thousand years old. But later investigations deeper down in the same soil came upon some more patterns, which were undoubtedly of Roman origin, and under these, a brick that bore ineffaceably the stamp of Mehemet Ali, a modern pasha.

If you have visited Minneapolis, you certainly must have been struck by the formation of the banks where the Mississippi has cut its way through the rocks. Above there is layer upon layer, stratum upon stratum of limestone, and beneath them the saccharoid sandstone, white as the sugar from which it derives its name, and soft enough to be cut with a knife, lies in huge masses. On the bluff overlooking the river, there lives, in an immense house, which many years ago was a popular hotel of the ancient city of St. Anthony's Falls, a friend of mine. One day there came to him startling news. Just outside of his premises, in excavating for the foundation of a new building, the workmen had struck upon a wooden coffin, and in it they found what was recognized to be, beyond all doubt, human bones. A local geologist, a physician of the state, with some skeptical tendencies, seized upon this new foundation of the antiquity of man, and the next day the columns of an evening paper of St. Paul contained an article from this gentleman's pen about what countless ages must have elapsed to perfect that saccharoid sandstone over the coffin, and over that to have put these layers upon layers of rock.

The conclusion was, that the chronology of the Bible was utterly a mistake, and that we had, before the days of Mr. Ingersoll, one of the mistakes of Moses. On reading the article my friend felt at once it was his duty to investigate the event. He found the coffin still unremoved, for it was solidly wedged into the saccharoid sandstone, and small pieces of the bones were scattered carelessly about. My friend, whose Christian feeling is only equaled by his profound ability and scholarship, began carefully to examine these relics of pre-Adamite man. Imagine his surprise to find that the coffin which had been made so many ages before Adam was placed upon this earth, was the plank sewer of the old hotel in which he lived, and the bones were those of some innocent lamb, that a careless cook had some time ago flung into that receptacle. I honor geology, but I claim it is yet a very imperfect science, and even with all its imperfections I have yet to find a solitary principle or fact that geology has laid down that contradicts one word of the five books of Moses.

A Mistake of Ingersoll, Tom Paine & Co. Corrected—Conclusion.

I allude to one more of the Mosaic facts that is assailed by the opponents of the Gospel. It is a difficulty which Mr. Ingersoll recently brought forward in that remarkable production of his, as something which he had discovered; but Bishop Colenso, whom the Church of England some thirty years ago sent out among the Zulus, dwelt upon it long ago, and even before his time, Tom Paine had made it his weapon against the truthfulness of the Pentateuch. It is simply this: We are told that the children of Israel, according to the Bible, were in the land of Egypt, in captivity, two hundred and fifteen years. There went down with Jacob and his sons, their wives and children, seventy souls in all. But the Exodus finds in the army of Israel six hundred thousand fighting men, involving a total of men, women and children which could not have been less than two or three millions, and it is declared that such an increase is utterly unparalleled in the annals of history. Our mathematicians have figured it all out to their satisfaction. Now, I want you to observe what a tissue of blunders make up this opposition to this Great Book. First of all turn back to the life of Abraham, the ancestor of Jacob, and you there discover that a Hebrew family did not consist merely of the parents and children. The servants were a part of the Hebrew household, and God distinctly made His commands imperative and unavoidable upon Abraham, that every male youth born in his house should receive the seal of circumcision. He therefore became a participator in the Abrahamic covenant. Nay, more, if he bought a servant he had to be brought into the covenant of circumcision. God insists upon this, and thus every servant of every Hebrew household became a Hebrew, and was reckoned in the family into which he was adopted. Away back in the time of Abraham, if you take up the Book of Genesis you will find he had so many of these servants born in his own household, that three hundred and eighteen of them, able-bodied men, soldiers, followed him to battle, and when Jacob, in the one hundred and thirtieth year of his age, went down into the land of Egypt the three hundred and eighteen of Abraham's day surely must have multiplied into thousands.

The Pentateuch, it is true, gives only the formal list of Jacob's sons, their wives and their children. There is no formal mention of this vast crowd of attendants, who, notwithstanding as part of the family, must have entered into the land of Egypt with them. Thus, at the very rate of increase that the tables of the census of the United States to-day display, these thousands might have easily amounted to three millions in two hundred and fifteen years.

I am not through with this stronghold of the enemies of the Pentateuch. As I study it seems to me that I never knew a ghost to vanish into thinner air. I would like to know where or how the critics learned that Israel was in bondage in the land of Egypt two hundred and fifteen years. Why, they learned in precisely the way that they learned that Moses said this earth was made just six thousand years ago. They have taken up certain genealogies and speculations of commentators. They have taken up the calculations of Hales and others, and they have regarded them as infallible. They have never turned to the twelfth chapter of Exodus, and I find there the statement given with precision that admits of no question that the sojourn of the children of Israel in Egypt was four hundred and thirty years: "And it came to pass, at the end of four hundred and thirty years, within the self-same day it came to pass that all the hosts of the Lord came out of the land of Egypt." Long before that, God had told Abraham that his seed should be strangers in a land that was not theirs, and that they should afflict them four hundred years. And the Jews so understood it, as shown by the fact that in the New Testament Stephen declares that God told the father of the faithful that his seed should sojourn in a strange land, and they should bring them into bondage and evil entreat them four hundred years. Now, if but seventy had gone down with Jacob into Egypt, an increase to two or three or even four millions in four and a half centuries would have been no more than what is paralleled by the history of every race on the surface of the globe.

In Italy, three hundred years ago, when men were wild over the discovery of Galileo's telescope, there was one philosopher who refused to look through the tube that pierced the vail of the starry worlds, and when he was asked the reason, "I am afraid," he said, "that I should believe Galileo's theory of the planetary motion." My brethren, look into the telescope of revelation. To know it, to study it, is to find the very truth of God.

Ingersoll's Lecture

on

SKULLS,

AND HIS

REPLIES TO PROF. SWING, DR. RYDER, DR. HERFORD, DR. COLLYER, AND OTHER CRITICS.

REPRINTED FROM "THE CHICAGO TIMES."

LADIES AND GENTLEMEN: Man advances just in the proportion that he mingles his thoughts with his labor — just in the proportion that he takes advantage of the forces of nature; just in proportion as he loses superstition and gains confidence in himself. Man advances as he ceases to fear the gods and learns to love his fellow-men. It is all, in my judgment, a question of intellectual development. Tell me the religion of any man and I will tell you the degree he marks on the intellectual thermometer of the world. It is a simple question of brain. Those among us who are the nearest barbarism have a barbarian religion. Those who are nearest civilization have the least superstition. It is, I say, a simple question of brain, and I want, in the first place, to lay the foundation to prove that assertion.

A little while ago I saw models of nearly everything that man has made. I saw models of all the water craft, from the rude dug-out in which floated a naked savage — one of our ancestors — a naked savage, with teeth twice as long as his forehead was high, with a spoonful of brains in the back of his orthodox head — I saw models of all the water craft of the world, from that dug-out up to a man-of-war that carries a hundred guns and miles of canvas; from that dug-out to the steamship that turns its brave prow from the port of New York, with a compass like a conscience, crossing three thousand miles of billows without missing a throb or beat of its mighty iron heart from shore to shore. And I saw at the same time the paintings of the world, from the rude daub of yellow mud to the landscapes that enrich palaces and adorn houses of what were once called the common people. I saw also their sculpture, from the rude god with four legs, a half dozen arms, several noses, and two or three rows of ears, and one little, contemptible, brainless head, up to the figures of to-day,—to the marbles that genius has clad in such a personality that it seems almost impudent to touch them without an introduction. I saw their books—books written upon the skins of wild beasts—upon shoulder-blades of sheep—books written upon leaves, upon bark, up to the splendid volumes that enrich the libraries of our day. When I speak of libraries I think of the remark of Plato: "A house that has a library in it has a soul."

I saw at the same time the offensive weapons that man has made, from a club, such as was grasped by that same savage when he crawled from his den in the ground and hunted a snake for his dinner: from that club to the boomerang, to the sword, to the cross-bow, to the blunderbuss, to the flint-lock, to the cap-lock, to the needle-gun, up to a cannon cast by Krupp, capable of hurling a ball weighing two thousand pounds through eighteen inches of solid steel. I saw, too, the armor from the shell of a turtle that one of our brave ancestors lashed upon his breast when he went to fight for his country; the skin of a porcupine, dried with the quills on, which this same savage pulled over his orthodox head, up to the shirts of mail that were worn in the middle ages, that laughed at the edge of the sword and defied the point of the spear; up to a monitor clad in complete steel. And I say orthodox not only in the matter of religion, but in everything. Whoever has quit growing he is orthodox, whether in art, politics, religion, philosophy—no matter what. Whoever thinks he has found it all out he is orthodox. Orthodoxy is that which rots, and heresy is that which grows forever. Orthodoxy is the night of the past, full of the darkness of superstition, and heresy is the eternal coming day, the light of which strikes the grand foreheads of the intellectual pioneers of the world. I saw their implements of agriculture, from the plow made of a crooked stick, atttached to the horn of an ox by some twisted straw, with which our ancestors scraped the earth, and from that to the agricultural implements of this generation, that make it possible for a man to cultivate the soil without being an ignoramus.

In the old time there was but one crop; and when the rain did not come in answer to the prayer of hypocrites a famine came and people fell upon their knees. At that time they were full of superstition. They were frightened all the time for fear that some god would be enraged at his poor, hapless, feeble and starving children. But now, instead of depending upon one crop they have several, and if there is not rain enough for one there may be enough for another. And if the frosts kill all, we have railroads and steamships enough to bring what we need from some other part of the world. Since man has found out something about agriculture, the gods have retired from the business of producing famines.

I saw at the same time their musical instruments, from the tom-tom —that is, a hoop with a couple of strings of raw-hide drawn across it— from that tom-tom, up to the instruments we have to-day, that make the common air blossom with melody, and I said to myself there is a regular advancement. I saw at the same time a row of human skulls, from the lowest skull that has been found, the Neanderthal skull— skulls from Central Africa, skulls from the bushmen of Australia— skulls from the farthest isles of the Pacific Sea—up to the best skulls of the last generation—and I noticed that there was the same difference between those skulls that there was between the *products* of those skulls, and I said to myself: "After all, it is a simple question of intellectual development." There was the same difference between those skulls, the lowest and highest skulls, that there was between the dug-out and the man-of-war and the steamship, between the club and the Krupp gun, between the yellow daub and the landscape, between the tom-tom and an opera by Verdi. The first and lowest skull in this row was the den in which crawled the base and meaner instincts of mankind, and the last was a temple in which dwelt joy, liberty and love. And I said to myself, it is all a question of intellectual development.

Man has advanced just as he has mingled his thought with his labor. As he has grown he has taken advantage of the forces of nature; first of the moving wind, then of falling water, and finally of steam. From one step to another he has obtained better houses, better clothes, and better books, and he has done it by holding out every incentive to the ingenious to produce them. The world has said, give us better clubs and guns and cannons with which to kill our fellow Christians. And whoever will give us better weapons and better music, and better houses to live in, we will robe him in wealth, crown him in honor, and render his name deathless. Every incentive was held out to every human being to improve these things, and that is the reason we have advanced in all mechanical arts. But that gentleman in the dug-out not only had his ideas about politics, mechanics, and agriculture; he had his ideas also about religion. His idea about politics was "right makes might." It will be thousands of years, may be, before mankind will believe in the saying that "right makes might." He had his religion. That low skull was a devil factory. He believed in Hell, and the belief was a consolation to him. He could see the waves of God's wrath dashing against the rocks of dark damnation. He could see tossing in the white-caps the faces of women, and stretching above the crests the dimpled hands of children; and he regarded these things as the justice and mercy of God. And all to-day who believe in this eternal punishment are the barbarians of the nineteenth century. That man believed in a devil, too, that had a long tail terminating with a fiery dart; that had wings like a bat—a devil that had a cheerful habit of breathing brimstone, that had a cloven foot, such as some orthodox clergymen seem to think I have. And there has not been a patentable improvement made upon that devil in all the years since. The moment you drive the devil out of theology, there is nothing left worth speaking of. The moment they drop the devil, away goes atonement. The moment they kill the devil, their whole scheme of salvation has lost all of its interest for mankind. You must keep the devil and you must keep Hell. You must keep the devil, because with no devil no priest is necessary. Now, all I ask is this—the same privilege to improve upon his religion as upon his dug-out, and that is what I am going to do, the best I can. No matter what church you belong to, or what church belongs to us. Let us be honor bright and fair.

I want to ask you: Suppose the king, if there was one, and the priest if there was one at that time, had told these gentlemen in the dug-out: "That dug-out is the best boat that can ever be built by man; the pattern of that came from on high, from the great God of storm and flood, and any man who says he can improve it by putting a stick in the middle of it and a rag on the stick, is an infidel, and shall be burned at the stake;" what, in your judgment—honor bright—would have been the effect upon the circumnavigation of the globe? Suppose the king, if there was one, and the priest, if there was one—and I presume there was a priest, because it was a very ignorant age—suppose this king and priest had said: "The tom-tom is the most beautiful instrument of music of which any man can conceive; that is the kind of music they have in Heaven; an angel sitting upon the edge of a glorified cloud, golden in the setting sun, playing upon that tom-tom, became so enraptured so entranced with her own music, that in a kind of ecstasy she dropped it—that is how we obtained it; and any man who says it can be improved by putting a back and front to it, and four strings, and a bridge, and getting a bow of hair with rosin, is a blaspheming wretch, and shall die the death,"—I ask you, what effect would that have had upon music? If that course had been pursued, would the human ears, in your judgment, ever have been enriched with the divine symphonies of Beethoven? Suppose the king, if there was one, and the priest, had said: "That crooked sticks is the best plow that can be invented; the pattern of that plow was given to a pious farmer in an exceedingly holy dream, and that twisted straw is the *ne plus ultra* of all twisted things, and any man who says he can make an improvement upon that plow, is an atheist;" what, in your judgment, would have been the effect upon the science of agriculture?

Now, all I ask is the same privilege to improve upon his religion as upon his mechanical arts. Why don't we go back to that period to get the telegraph? Because they were barbarians. And shall we go to barbarians to get our religion? What is religion? Religion simply embraces the duty of man to man. Religion is simply the science of human duty and the duty of man to man—that is what it is. It is the highest science of all. And all other sciences are as nothing, except as they contribute to the happiness of man. The science of religion is the highest of all, embracing all others. And shall we go to the barbarians to learn the science of sciences? The nineteenth century knows more about religion than all the centuries dead. There is more real charity in the world to-day than ever before. There is more thought to-day than ever before. Woman is glorified to-day as she never was before in the history of the world. There are more happy families now than ever before—more children treated as though they were tender blossoms than as though they were brutes than in any other time or nation. Religion is simply the duty a man owes to man; and when you fall upon your knees and pray for something you know not of, you neither benefit the one you pray for nor yourself. One ounce of restitution is worth a million of repentances anywhere, and a man will get along faster by helping himself a minute than by praying ten years for somebody to help him. Suppose you were coming along the street, and found a party of men and women on their knees praying to a bank, and you asked them, " Have any of you borrowed any money of this bank?" " No, but our fathers, they, too, prayed to this bank." " Did they ever get any?" " No, not that we ever heard of." I would tell them to get up. It is easier to earn it, and it is far more manly.

Our fathers in the " good old times,"—and the best that I can say of the " good old times " is that they are gone, and the best I can say of the good old people that lived in them is that they are gone, too—believed that you made a man think your way by force. Well, you can't do it. There is a splendid something in man that says: " I won't; I won't be driven." But our fathers thought men could be driven. They tried it in the " good old times." I used to read about the manner in which the early Christians made converts—how they impressed upon the world the idea that God loved them. I have read it, but it didn't burn into my soul. I didn't think much about it—I heard so much about being fried forever in Hell that it didn't seem so bad to burn a few minutes. I love liberty and I hate all persecutions in the name of God. I never appreciated the infamies that have been committed in the name of religion until I saw the iron arguments that Christians used. I saw, for instance, the thumb-screw, two little innocent looking pieces of iron, armed with some little protuberances on the inner side to keep it from slipping down, and through each end a screw, and when some man had made some trifling remark, as, for instance, that he never believed that God made a fish swallow a man to keep him from drowning, or something like that, or, for instance, that he didn't believe in baptism. You know that is very wrong. You can see for yourselves the justice of damning a man if his parents had happened to baptize him in the wrong way— God can not afford to break a rule or two to save all the men in the world. I happened to be in the company of some Baptist ministers once—you may wonder how I happened to be in such company as that— and one of them asked me what I thought about baptism. Well, I told them I hadn't thought much about it—that I had never sat up nights on that question. I said: "Baptism—with soap—is a good institution." Now, when some man had said some trifling thing like that, they put this thumb-screw on him, and in the name of universal benevolence and for the love of God—man has never persecuted man for the love of man; man has never persecuted another for the love of charity—it is always for the love of something he calls God, and every man's idea of God is his own idea. If there is an infinite God, and there may be—I don't know—there may be a million for all I know—I hope there is more than one—one seems so lonesome. They kept turning this down, and when this was done, most men would say: "I will recant." I think I would. There is not much of the martyr about me. I would have told them: "Now you write it down, and I will sign it. You may have one God or a million, one Hell or a million. You stop that—I am tried."

Do you know, sometimes I have thought that all the hypocrites in the world are not worth one drop of honest blood. I am sorry that any good man ever died for religion. I would rather let them advance a little easier. It is too bad to see a good man sacrificed for a lot of wild beasts and cattle. But there is now and then a man who would not swerve the breadth of a hair. There was now and then a sublime heart willing to die for an intellectual conviction, and had it not been for these men we would have been wild beasts and savages to-day. There were some men who would not take it back, and had it not been for a few such brave, heroic souls in every age we would have been cannibals, with pictures of wild beasts tattooed upon our breasts, dancing around some dried-snake fetish. And so they turned it down to the last thread of agony, and threw the victim into some dungeon, where, in the throb.

bing silence and darkness, he might suffer the agonies of the fabled damned. This was done in the name of love, in the name of mercy, in the name of the compassionate Christ. And the men that did it are the men that made our Bible for us.

I saw, too, at the same time, the collar of torture. Imagine a circle of iron, and on the inside a hundred points almost as sharp as needles. This argument was fastened about the throat of the sufferer. Then he could not walk nor sit down, nor stir without the neck being punctured by these points. In a little while the throat would begin to swell, and suffocation would end the agonies of that man. This man, it may be, had committed the crime of saying, with tears upon his cheeks, "I do not believe that God, the father of us all, will damn to eternal perdition any of the children of men." And that was done to convince the world that God so loved the world that He died for us. That was in order that people might hear the glad tidings of great joy to all people.

I saw another instrument, called the scavenger's daughter. Imagine a pair of shears with handles, not only where they now are, but at the points as well and just above the pivot that unites the blades a circle of iron. In the upper handles the hands would be placed; in the lower, the feet; and through the iron ring, at the centre, the head of the victim would be forced, and in that position the man would be thrown upon the earth, and the strain upon the muscle would produce such agony that insanity took pity. And this was done to keep people from going to Hell—to convince that man that he had made a mistake in his logic— and it was done, too, by Protestants—Protestants that persecuted to the extent of their power, and that is as much as Catholicism ever did. They would persecute now if they had the power. There is not a man in this vast audience who will say that the church should have temporal power. There is not one of you but what believes in the eternal divorce of church and state. Is it possible that the only people who are fit to go to heaven are the only people not fit to rule mankind?

I saw at the same time the rack. This was a box like the bed of a wagon, with a windlass at each end, and ratchets to prevent slipping. Over each windlass went chains, and when some man had, for instance, denied the doctrine of the trinity, a doctrine it is necessary to believe in order to get to Heaven — but, thank the Lord, you don't have to understand it. This man merely denied that three times one was one, or maybe he denied that there was ever any Son in the world exactly as old as his father, or that there ever was a boy eternally older than his mother—then they put that man on the rack. Nobody had ever been persecuted for calling God bad—it has always been for calling him good. When I stand here to say that, if there is a Hell, God is a fiend; they say that is very bad. They say I am trying to tear down the institutions of public virtue. But let me tell you one thing; there is no reformation in fear — you can scare a man so that he won't do it sometimes, but I will swear you can't scare him so bad that he won't want to do it. Then they put this man on the rack and priests began turning these levers, and kept turning until the ankles, the hips, the shoulders, the elbows, the wrists, and all the joints of the victim were dislocated, and he was wet with agony, and standing by was a physician to feel his pulse. What for? To save his life? Yes. In mercy? No. But in order that they might have the pleasure of racking him once more. And this was the Christian spirit. This was done in the name of civilization, in the name of religion, and all these wretches who did it died in peace. There is not an orthodox preacher in the city that has not a respect for every one of them. As, for instance, for John Calvin, who was a murderer and nothing but a murderer, who would have disgraced an ordinary gallows by being hanged upon it. These men when they came to die were not frightened. God did not send any devils into their death-rooms to make mouths at them. He reserved them for Voltaire, who brought religious liberty to France. He reserved them for Thomas Paine, who did more for liberty than all the churches. But all the inquisitors died with the white hands of peace folded over the breast of piety. And when they died, the room was filled with the rustle of the wings of angels, waiting to bear the wretches to Heaven.

When I read these frightful books it seems to me sometimes as though I had suffered all these things myself. It seems sometimes as though I had stood upon the shore of exile, and gazed with tearful eyes toward home and native land; it seems to me as though I had been staked out upon the sands of the sea, and drowned by the inexorable, advancing tide; as though my nails had been torn from my hands, and into the bleeding quick needles had been thrust; as though my feet had been crushed in iron boots; as though I had been chained in the cell of the Inquisition, and listened with dying ears for the coming footsteps of release; as though I had stood upon the scaffold and saw the glittering axe fall upon me; as though I had been upon the rack and had seen, bending above me, the white faces of hypocrite priests; as though I had been taken from my fireside, from my wife and children, taken to the public square, chained; as though fagots had been piled about me; as though the flames had climbed around my limbs and scorched my eyes to blindness, and as though my ashes had been scattered to the four winds by all the countless hands of hate. And, while I so feel, I swear that while I live I will do what little I can to augment the liberties of man, woman and child. I denounce slavery and superstition everywhere. I believe in liberty, and happiness, and love, and joy in this world. I am amazed that any man ever had the impudence to try and do another man's thinking. I have just as good a right to talk about theology as a minister. If they all agreed I might admit it was a science, but as they all disagree, and the more they study the wider they get apart, I may be permitted to suggest it is not a science. When no two will tell you the road to Heaven—that is, giving you the same route —and if you would inquire of them all, you would just give up trying to go there, and say: "I may as well stay where I am, and let the Lord come to me."

Do you know that this world has not been fit for a lady and gentleman to live in for twenty-five years, just on account of slavery. It was not until the year 1808 that Great Britain abolished the slave trade, and up to that time her judges, her priests occupying her pulpits, the members of the royal family, owned stock in the slave ships, and luxuriated upon the profits of piracy and murder. It was not until the same year that the United States of America abolished the slave trade between this and other countries, but carefully preserved it as between the states. It was not until the 28th day of August, 1833, that Great Britain abolished human slavery in her colonies; and it was not until the 1st day of January, 1863, that Abraham Lincoln, sustained by the sublime and heroic North, rendered our flag pure as the sky in which it floats. Abraham Lincoln was, in my judgment, in many respects, the grandest man ever president of the United States. Upon his monument these words should be written: "Here sleeps the only man in the history of the world, who, having been clothed with almost absolute power, never abused it, except upon the side of mercy."

For two hundred years the Christians of the United States deliberately turned the cross of Christ into a whipping-post. Christians bred hounds to catch other Christians. Let me show you what the Bible has done for mankind: "Servants, be obedient to your masters." The only word coming from that sweet Heaven was, "Servants, obey your masters." Frederick Douglas told me that he had lectured upon the subject of freedom twenty years before he was permitted to set his foot in a church. I tell you the world has not been fit to live in for twenty-five years. Then all the people used to cringe and crawl to preachers. Mr. Buckle, in his history of civilization, shows that men were even struck dead for speaking impolitely to a priest. God would not stand it. See how they used to crawl before cardinals, bishops and popes. It is not so now. Before wealth they bowed to the very earth, and in the presence of titles they became abject. All this is slowly, but surely changing. We no longer bow to men simply because they are rich. Our fathers worshipped the golden calf. The worst you can say of an American now is, he worships the gold of the calf. Even the calf is beginning to see this distinction.

The time will come when no matter how much money a man has, he will not be respected unless he is using it for the benefit of his fellow-men. It will soon be here. It no longer satisfies the ambition of a great man to be king or emperor. The last Napoleon was not satisfied with being the emperor of the French. He was not satisfied with having a circlet of gold about his head. He wanted some evidence that he had something of value within his head. So he wrote the life of Julius Cæsar, that he might become a member of the French academy. The emperors, the kings, the popes, no longer tower above their fellows. Compare, for instance, King William and Helmholtz. The king is one of the anointed by the Most High, as they claim—one upon whose head has been poured the divine petroleum of authority. Compare this king with Helmholtz, who towers an intellectual Colossus above the crowned mediocrity. Compare George Eliot with Queen Victoria. The queen is clothed in garments given her by blind fortune and unreasoning chance, while George Eliot wears robes of glory woven in the loom of her own genius. And so it is the world over. The time is coming when a man will be rated at his real worth, and that by his brain and heart. We care nothing now about an officer unless he fills his place. No matter if he is president, if he rattles in the place nobody cares anything about him. I might give you an instance in point, but I won't. The world is getting better and grander and nobler every day.

Now, if men have been slaves, if they have crawled in the dust before one another, what shall I say of women? They have been the slaves of men. It took thousands of ages to bring women from abject slavery up to the divine height of marriage. I believe in marriage. If there is any Heaven upon earth it is in the family by the fireside, and the family is a unit of government. Without the family relation is tender, pure and true, civilization is impossible. Ladies, the ornaments you wear upon your persons to-night are but the souvenirs of your mother's bondage. The chains around your necks, and the bracelets clasped upon your white arms by the thrilled hand of love, have been changed by the wand of civilization from iron to shining, glittering gold. Nearly every civilization in this world accounts for the devilment in it by the crimes of woman. They say woman brought all the trouble into the world. I don't care if she did. I would rather live in a world full of trouble with the women I love, than to live in Heaven with nobody but men. I read in a book an account of the creation of the world. The book I have taken pains to say was not written by any God. And why do I say so? Because I can write a far better book myself. Because it is full of barbarisms. Several ministers in this city have undertaken to answer me —notably those who don't believe the Bible themselves. I want to ask

Every minister in the City of Chicago that answers me, and those who have answered me had better answer me again — I want them to say, and without any sort of evasion — without resorting to any pious tricks — I want them to say whether they believe that the Eternal God of this universe ever upheld the crime of polygamy. Say it square and fair. Don't begin to talk about that being a peculiar time, and that God was easy on the prejudices of those old fellows. I want them to answer that question and to answer it squarely, which they haven't done. Did this God, which you pretend to worship, ever sanction the institution of human slavery? Now, answer fair? Don't slide around it. Don't begin and answer what a bad man I am, nor what a good man Moses was. Stick to the text. Do you believe in a God that allowed a man to be sold from his children? Do you worship such an infinite monster? And if you do, tell your congregation whether you are not ashamed to admit it. Let every minister who answers me again tell whether he believes God commanded his general to kill the little dimpled babe in the cradle. Let him answer it. Don't say that those were very bad times. Tell whether He did it or not, and then your people will know whether to hate that God or not. Be honest. Tell them whether that God in war captured young maidens and turned them over to the soldiers; and then ask the wives and sweet girls of your congregation to get down on their knees and worship the infinite fiend that did that thing. Answer! It is your God I am talking about, and if that is what God did, please tell your congregation what, under the same circumstances, the devil would have done. Don't tell your people that is a poem. Don't tell your people that is pictorial. That won't do. Tell your people whether it is true or false. That is what I want you to do.

In this book I have read about God's making the world and one man. That is all he intended to make. The making of woman was a second thought, though I am willing to admit that as a rule second thoughts are best. This God made a man and put him in a public park. In a little while He noticed that the man got lonesome; then He found He had made a mistake, and that He would have to make somebody to keep him company. But having used up all the nothing He originally used in making the world and one man, He had to take a part of a man to start a woman with. So He causes sleep to fall on this man—now understand me, I do not say this story is true. After the sleep had fallen on this man the Supreme Being took a rib, or, as the French would call it, a cutlett, out of him, and from that He made a woman; and I am willing to swear, taking into account the amount and quality of the raw material used, this was the most magnificent job ever accomplished in this world. Well, after He got the woman done she was brought to the man, not to see how she liked him, but to see how he liked her. He liked her and they started housekeeping, and they were told of certain things they might do and of one thing they could not do—and of course they did it. I would have done it in fifteen minutes, I know it. There wouldn't have been an apple on that tree half an hour from date, and the limbs would have been full of clubs. And then they were turned out of the park and extra policemen were put on to keep them from getting back. And then trouble commenced and we have been at it ever since. Nearly all of the religions of this world account for the existence of evil by such a story as that.

Well, I read in another book what appeared to be an account of the same transaction. It was written about four thousand years before the other. All commentators agree that the one that was written last was the original, and the one that was written first was copied from the one that was written last. But I would advise you all not to allow your creed to be disturbed by a little matter of four or five thousand years. It is a great deal better to be mistaken in dates than to go to the devil. In this other account the Supreme Brahma made up his mind to make the world and a man and woman. He made the world, and he made the man and then the woman, and put them on the Island of Ceylon. According to the account it was the most beautiful island of which man can conceive. Such birds, such songs, such flowers, and such verdure! And the branches of the trees were so arranged that when the wind swept through them every tree was a thousand Eolian harps. Brahma, when he put them there, said: "Let them have a period of courtship, for it is my desire and will that true love should forever precede marriage." When I read that, it was so much more beautiful and lofty than the other, that I said to myself: "If either one of these stories ever turns out to be true, I hope it will be this one."

Then they had their courtship, with the nightingale singing and the stars shining and the flowers blooming, and they fell in love. Imagine that courtship! No prospective fathers or mothers-in-law; no prying and gossiping neighbors; nobody to say, "Young man, how do you expect to support her?" Nothing of that kind—nothing but the nightingale singing its song of joy and pain, as though the thorn already touched its heart. They were married by the Supreme Brahma, and he said to them, "Remain here; you must never leave this island." Well, after a little while the man—and his name was Adami, and the woman's name was Heva—said to Heva: "I believe I'll look about a little." He wanted to go West. He went to the western extremity of the island where there was a little narrow neck of land connecting it with the mainland, and the Devil, who is always playing pranks with us, produced a mirage, and when he looked over to the mainland, such hills and vales, such dells and dales, such mountains crowned with snow, such cataracts clad in bows of glory did he see there, that he went back and told Heva: "The country over there is a thousand times better than this; let us migrate." She, like every other woman that ever lived, said: "Let well enough alone; we have all we want; let us stay here." But he said: "No, let us go;" so she followed him, and when they came to this narrow neck of land, he took her on his back like a gentleman, and carried her over. But the moment they got over they heard a crash, and, looking back, discovered that this narrow neck of land had fallen into the sea. The mirage had disappeared, and there was naught but rocks and sand, and then the Supreme Brahma cursed them both to the lowest Hell.

Then it was that the man spoke—and I have liked him ever since for it—"Curse me, but curse not her; it was not her fault, it was mine." That's the kind of a man to start a world with. The Supreme Brahma said: "I will save her but not thee." And then spoke out of her fullness of love, out of a heart in which there was love enough to make all her daughters rich in holy affection, and said: "If thou wilt not spare him, spare neither me; I do not wish to live without him, I love him." Then the Supreme Brahma said—and I have liked him ever since I read it—"I will spare you both, and watch over you and your children forever." Honor bright, is that not the better and grander story?

And in that same book I find this: "Man is strength, woman is beauty; man is courage, woman is love. When the one man loves the one woman, and the one woman loves the one man, the very angels leave Heaven, and come and sit in that house, and sing for joy." In the same book this: "Blessed is that man, and beloved of all the gods, who is afraid of no man, and of whom no man is afraid." Magnificent character! A missionary certainly ought to talk to that man. And I find this: "Never will I accept private, individual salvation, but rather will I stay and work, strive and suffer, until every soul from every star has been brought home to God." Compare that with the Christian that expects to go to Heaven while the world is rolling over Niagara to an eternal and unending Hell. So I say that religion lays all the crime and troubles of this world at the beautiful feet of woman. And then the church has the impudence to say that it has exalted women. I believe that marriage is a perfect partnership; that woman has every right that man has—and one more—the right to be protected. Above all men in the world I hate a stingy man—a man that will make his wife beg for money. "What did you do with the dollar I gave you last week?" "And what are you going to do with this?" It is vile. No gentleman will ever be satisfied with the love of a beggar and a slave—no gentleman will ever be satisfied except with the love of an equal. What kind of children does a man expect to have with a beggar for their mother? A man can not be so poor but that he can be generous, and if you only have one dollar in the world and you have got to spend it, spend it like a lord—spend it as though it were a dry leaf, and you the owner of unbounded forests—spend it as though you had a wilderness of your own. That's the way to spend it.

I had rather be a beggar and spend my last dollar like a king, than be a king and spend my money like a beggar. If it has got to go let it go. And this is my advice to the poor. For you can never be so poor that whatever you do you can't do in a grand and manly way. I hate a cross man. What right has a man to assassinate the joy of life? When you go home you ought to go like a ray of light—so that it will, even in the night, burst out of the doors and windows and illuminate the darkness. Some men think their mighty brains have been in a turmoil; they have been thinking about who will be Alderman from the Fifth Ward; they have been thinking about politics, great and mighty questions have been engaging their minds, they have bought calico at five cents or six, and want to sell it for seven. Think of the intellectual strain that must have been upon that man, and when he gets home everybody else in the house must look out for his comfort. A woman who has only taken care of five or six children, and one or two of them sick, has been nursing them and singing to them, and trying to make one yard of cloth do the work of two, she, of course, is fresh and fine and ready to wait upon this gentleman—the head of the family—the boss!

I was reading the other day of an apparatus invented for the ejectment of gentlemen who subsist upon free lunches. It is so arranged that when the fellow gets both hands into the victuals, a large hand descends upon him, jams his hat over his eyes—he is seized, turned toward the door, and just in the nick of time an immense boot comes from the other side, kicks him in italics, sends him out over the sidewalk and lands him rolling in the gutter. I never hear of such a man—a boss—that I don't feel as though that machine ought to be brought into requisition for his benefit.

Love is the only thing that will pay ten per cent of interest on the outlay. Love is the only thing in which the height of extravagance is the last degree of economy. It is the only thing, I tell you. Joy is wealth. Love is the legal tender of the soul—and you need not be rich to be happy. We have all been raised on success in this country. Always been talked with about being successful, and have never thought ourselves very rich unless we were the possessors of some magnificent mansion, and unless our names have been between the putrid lips of rumor we could not be happy. Every little boy is striving to be this and be that. I tell you the happy man is the successful man. The man that has won the love of one good woman is a successful man. The man that has been the emperor of one good heart, and that heart embraced all his, has been a success. If another has been the emperor of the round world and has never loved and been loved, his life is a failure. It won't do. Let us teach our children the other way, that the happy man is the successful man, and he who is a happy man is the one who always tries to make some one else happy.

The man who marries a woman to make her happy; that marries her as much for her own sake as for his own; not the man that thinks his wife is his property, who thinks that the title to her belongs to him—that the woman is the property of the man; wretches who get mad at their wives and then shoot them down in the street because they think the woman is their property. I tell you it is not necessary to be rich and great and powerful to be happy.

A little while ago I stood by the grave of the old Napoleon—a magnificent tomb of gilt and gold, fit almost for a dead deity—and gazed upon the sarcophagus of black Egyptian marble, where rest at last the ashes of the restless man. I leaned over the balustrade and thought about the career of the greatest soldier of the modern world. I saw him walking upon the banks of the Seine, contemplating suicide—I saw him at Toulon—I saw him putting down the mob in the streets of Paris—I saw him at the head of the army of Italy—I saw him crossing the bridge of Lodi with the tri-color in his hand—I saw him in Egypt in the shadows of the pyramids—I saw him conquer the Alps and mingle the eagles of France with the eagles of the crags. I saw him at Marengo—at Ulm and Asterlitz. I saw him in Russia, where the infantry of the snow and the cavalry of the wild blast scattered his legions like Winter's withered leaves. I saw him at Leipsic in defeat and disaster—driven by a million bayonets back upon Paris—clutched like a wild beast—banished to Elba. I saw him escape and retake an empire by the force of his genius. I saw him upon the frightful field of Waterloo, where chance and fate combined to wreck the fortunes of their former king. And I saw him at St. Helena, with his hands crossed behind him, gazing out upon the sad and solemn sea. I thought of the orphans and widows he had made—of the tears that had been shed for his glory, and of the only woman who ever loved him, pushed from his heart by the cold hand of ambition. And I said I would rather have been a French peasant and worn wooden shoes. I would rather have lived in a hut with a vine growing over the door, and the grapes growing purple in the kisses of the Autumn sun. I would rather have been that poor peasant with my loving wife by my side, knitting as the day died out of the sky—with my children upon my knees and their arms about me. I would rather have been that man and gone down to the tongueless silence of the dreamless dust, than to have been that imperial impersonation of force and murder known as Napoleon the Great. It is not necessary to be rich in order to be happy. It is only necessary to be in love. Thousands of men go to college and get a certificate that they have an education, and that certificate is in Latin and they stop studying, and in two years to save their life they couldn't read the certificate they got.

It is mostly so in marrying. They stop courting when they get married. They think, we have won her and that is enough. Ah! the difference before and after! How well they look! How bright their eyes! How light their steps, and how full they were of generosity and laughter! I tell you a man should consider himself in good luck if a woman loves him when he is doing his level best! Good luck! Good luck! And another thing that is the cause of much trouble is that people don't count fairly. They do what they call putting their best foot forward. That means lying a little. I say put your worst foot forward. If you have got any faults admit them. If you drink, say so and quit it. If you chew and smoke and swear, say so. If some of your kindred are not very good people, say so. If you have had two or three that died on the gallows, or that ought to have died there, say so. Tell all your faults, and if after she knows your faults she says she will have you, you have got the dead wood on that woman forever. I claim that there should be perfect equality in the home, and I can not think of anything nearer Heaven than a home where there is true republicanism and true democracy at the fireside. All are equal.

And then, do you know, I like to think that love is eternal; that if you really love the woman, for her sake, you will love her no matter what she may do; that if she really loves you, for your sake, the same; that love does not look at alterations, through the wrinkles of time, through the mask of years—if you really love her you will always see the face you loved and won. And I like to think of it. If a man loves a woman she does not ever grow old to him, and the woman who really loves a man does not see that he grows old. He is not decrepit to her. He is not tremulous. He is not old. He is not bowed. She always sees the same gallant fellow that won her hand and heart. I like to think of it in that way, and as Shakspeare says: "Let Time reach with his sickle as far as ever he can; although he can reach ruddy cheeks and ripe lips, and flashing eyes, he can not quite reach love." I like to think of it. We will go down the hill of life together, and enter the shadow one with the other, and as we go down we may hear the ripple of the laughter of our grandchildren, and the birds, and spring, and youth, and love will sing once more upon the leafless branches of the tree of age.

I love to think of it in that way—absolute equals, happy, happy, and free, all our own.

But some people say: "Would you allow a woman to vote?" Yes, if she wants to; that is her business, not mine. If a woman wants to vote, I am too much of a gentleman to say she shall not. But they say woman has not sense enough to vote. It don't take much. But it seems to me there are some questions, as for instance, the question of peace and war, that a woman should be allowed to vote upon. A woman that has sons to be offered on the altar of that Moloch, it seems to me that such a grand woman should have as much right to vote upon the question of peace and war as some thrice-besotted sot that reels to the ballot box and deposits his vote for war. But if women have been slaves, what shall we say of the little children born in the sub-cellars; children of poverty, children of crime, children of wealth, children that are afraid when they hear their names pronounced by the lips of the mother, children that cower in fear when they hear the footsteps of their brutal father, the flotsam and jetsam upon the rude sea of life, my heart goes out to them one and all.

Children have all the rights that we have and one more, and that is to be protected. Treat your children in that way. Suppose your child tells a lie. Don't pretend that the whole world is going into bankruptcy. Don't pretend that that is the first lie ever told. Tell them, like an honest man, that you have told hundreds of lies yourself, and tell the dear little darling that it is not the best way; that it soils the soul. Think of the man that deals in stocks whipping his children for putting false rumors afloat! Think of an orthodox minister whipping his own flesh and blood, for not telling all it thinks! Think of that! Think of a lawyer beating his child for avoiding the truth! when the old man makes about half his living that way. A lie is born of weakness on one side and tyranny on the other. That is what it is. Think of a great big man coming at a little bit of a child with a club in his hand! What is the little darling to do? Lie, of course. I think that mother Nature put that ingenuity into the mind of the child, when attacked by a parent, to throw up a little breastwork in the shape of a lie to defend itself. When a great general wins a battle by what they call strategy, we build monuments to him. What is strategy? Lies. Suppose a man as much larger than we are as we are larger than a child five years of age, should come at us with a liberty pole in his hand, and in tones of thunder want to know "who broke that plate," there isn't one of us, not excepting myself, that wouldn't swear that we never had seen that plate in our lives, or that it was cracked when we got it.

Another good way to make children tell the truth is to tell it yourself. Keep your word with your child the same as you would with your banker. If you tell a child you will do anything, either do it or give the child the reason why. Truth is born of confidence. It comes from the lips of love and liberty. I was over in Michigan the other day. There was a boy over there at Grand Rapids about five or six years old, a nice, smart boy, as you will see from the remark he made—what you might call a nineteenth century boy. His father and mother had promised to take him out riding. They had promised to take him out riding for about three weeks, and they would slip off and go without him. Well, after a while, that got kind of played out with the little boy, and the day before I was there they played the trick on him again. They went out and got the carriage, and went away, and as they rode away from the front of the house, he happened to be standing there with his nurse, and he saw them. The whole thing flashed on him in a moment. He took in the situation, and turned to his nurse and said, pointing to his father and mother: "There goes the two d——t liars in the State of Michigan!" When you go home fill the house with joy, so that the light of it will stream out the windows and doors, and illuminate even the darkness. It is just as easy that way as any in the world.

I want to tell you to-night that you can not get the robe of hypocrisy on you so thick that the sharp eye of childhood will not see through every veil, and if you pretend to your children that you are the best man that ever lived—the bravest man that ever lived—they will find you out every time. They will not have the same opinion of father when they grow up that they used to have. They will have to be in mighty bad luck if they ever do meaner things than you have done. When your child confesses to you that it has committed a fault, take that child in your arms, and let it feel your heart beat against its heart, and raise your children in the sunlight of love, and they will be sunbeams to you along the pathway of life. Abolish the club and the whip from the house, because, if the civilized use a whip, the ignorant and the brutal will use a club, and they will use it because you use the whip.

Every little while some door is thrown open in some orphan asylum, and there we see the bleeding back of a child whipped beneath the roof that was raised by love. It is infamous, and the man that can't raise a child without the whip ought not to have a child. If there is one of you here that ever expect to whip your child again, let me ask you something. Have your photograph taken at the time and let it show your face red with vulgar anger, and the face of the little one with eyes swimming in tears, and the little chin dimpled with fear, looking like a piece of water struck by a sudden cold wind. If that little child should die, I can not think of a sweeter way to spend an Autumn afternoon than to take that photograph and go to the cemetery, when the maples are clad in tender gold, and when little scarlet runners are coming from the sad heart of the earth, and sit down upon that mound, and look upon that photograph, and think of the flesh, now dust, that you beat. Just think of it. I could not bear to die in the arms of a child that I had whipped. I could not bear to feel upon my lips, when they were withered beneath the touch of death, the kiss of one that I had struck. Some Christians act as though they really thought that when Christ said, "Suffer little children to come unto me," He had a rawhide under His coat. They act as though they really thought that He made that remark simply to get the children within striking distance.

I have known Christians to turn their children from their doors, especially a daughter, and then get down on their knees and pray to God to watch over them and help them. I will never ask God to help my children unless I am doing my level best in that same wretched line. I will tell you what I say to my girls: "Go where you will; do what crime you may; fall to what depth of degradation you may; in all the storms and winds and earthquakes of life, no matter what you do, you never can commit any crime that will shut my door, my arms or my heart to you. As long as I live you shall have one sincere friend." Call me an antheist; call me an infidel because I hate the God of the Jew— which I do. I intend so to live that when I die my children can come to my grave and truthfully say: "He who sleeps here never gave us one moment of pain."

When I was a boy there was one day in each week too good for a child to be happy in. In these good old times Sunday commenced when the sun went down on Saturday night, and closed when the sun went down on Sunday night. We commenced Saturday to get a good ready. And when the sun went down Saturday night there was a gloom deeper than midnight that fell upon the house. You could not crack hickory nuts then. And if you were caught chewing gum, it was only another evidence of the total depravity of the human heart. Well, after a while we got to bed sadly and sorrowfully after having heard Heaven thanked that we were not all in Hell. And I sometimes used to wonder how the mercy of God lasted as long as it did, because I recollected that on several occasions I had not been at school, when I was supposed to be there. Why I was not burned to a crisp was a mystery to me. The next morning we got up and we got ready for church—all solemn, and when we got there the minister was up in the pulpit, about twenty feet high, and he commenced at Genesis about "The fall of man," and he went on to about twenty thirdly; then he struck the second application, and when he struck the application I knew he was about half way through. And then he went on to show the scheme how the Lord was satisfied by punishing the wrong man. Nobody but a God would have thought of that ingenious way. Well, when he got through that, then came the catechism

—the chief end of man. Then my turn came, and we sat along on a little bench where our feet came within about fifteen inches of the floor, and the dear old minister used to ask us:

"Boys, do you know that you ought to be in Hell?"

And we answered up as cheerfully as could be expected under the circumstances:

"Yes, sir."

"Well, boys, do you know that you would go to Hell if you died in your sins?"

And we said: "Yes, sir."

And then came the great test:

"Boys"—I can't get the tone, you know. And do you know that is how the preachers get the bronchitis. You never heard of an auctioneer getting the bronchitis, nor the second mate on a steamboat—never. What gives it to the minister is talking solemnly when they don't feel that way, and it has the same influence upon the organs of speech that it would have upon the cords of the calves of your legs to walk on your tip-toes, and so I call bronchitis "parsonitis." And if the ministers would all tell exactly what they think they would all get well, but keeping back a part of the truth is what gives them bronchitis.

Well the old man—the dear old minister—used to try and show us how long we would be in Hell if we would only locate there. But to finish the other. The grand test question was:

"Boys, if it was God's will that you should go to Hell, would you be willing to go?"

And every little liar said:

"Yes, sir."

Then, in order to tell how long we would stay there, he used to say:

"Suppose once in a billion ages a bird should come from a far distant clime and carry off in its bill one little grain of sand, the time would finally come when the last grain of sand would be carried away. Do you understand?

"Yes, sir."

"Boys, by that time it would not be sun-up in Hell."

Where did that doctrine of Hell come from? I will tell you; from that fellow in the dug-out. Where did he get it? It was a souvenir from the wild beasts. Yes, I tell you he got it from the wild beasts, from the glittering eye of the serpent, from the coiling, twisting snakes with their fangs mouths; and it came from the bark, growl and howl of wild beasts; it was born of a laugh of the hyena and got it from the depraved chatter of malicious apes. And I despise it with every drop of my blood and defy it. If there is any God in this universe who will damn his children for an expression of an honest thought I wish to go to Hell. I would rather go there than go to Heaven and keep the company of a God that would thus damn his children. Oh! it is an infamous doctrine to teach that to little children, to put a shadow in the heart of a child to fill the insane asylums with that miserable, infamous lie. I see now and then a little girl—a dear little darling, with a face like the light, and eyes of joy, a human blossom, and I think, "is it possible that little girl will ever grow up to be a Presbyterian?" Is it possible, my goodness, that that flower will finally believe in the five points of Calvinism or in the eternal damnation of man?" Is it possible that that little fairy will finally believe that she could be happy in Heaven with her baby in Hell? Think of it! Think of it! And that is the Christian religion!

We cry out against the Indian mother that throws her child into the Ganges to be devoured by the alligator or crocodile, but that is joy in comparison with the Christian mother's hope, that she may be in salvation while her brave boy is in Hell.

I tell you I want to kick the doctrine about Hell—I want to kick it out every time I go by it. I want to get Americans in this country placed so they will be ashamed to preach it. I want to get the congregations so that they won't listen to it. We can not divide the world off into saints and sinners in that way. There is a little girl, fair as a flower, and she grows up until she is twelve, thirteen, or fourteen years old. Are you going to damn her in the fifteenth, sixteenth or seventeenth year, when the arrow from Cupid's bow touches her heart and she is glorified—are you going to damn her now? She marries and loves, and holds in her arms a beautiful child. Are you going to damn her now? When are you going to damn her? Because she has listened to some Methodist minister and after all that flood of light failed to believe? Are you going to damn her then? I tell you God can not afford to damn such a woman.

A woman in the State of Indiana forty or fifty years ago who carded the wool and made rolls and spun them, and made the cloth and cut out the clothes for the children, and nursed them, and sat up with them nights and gave them medicine, and held them in her arms and wept over them—cried for joy and wept for fear, and finally raised ten or eleven good men and women with the ruddy glow of health upon their cheeks, and she would have died for any one of them any moment of her life, and finally she, bowed with age and bent with care and labor, dies, and at the moment the magical touch of death is upon her face, she looks as though she never had had a care, and her children burying her cover her face with tears. Do you tell me God can afford to damn that kind of a woman? One such act of injustice would turn Heaven itself into Hell. If there is any God, sitting above him in infinite serenity we have the figure of justice. Even a God must do justice; even a God must worship justice; and any form of superstition that destroys justice is infamous! Just think of teaching that doctrine to little children! A little child would go out into the garden, and there would be a little tree laden with blossoms, and the little fellow would lean against it, and there would be a bird on one of the bows, singing and swinging, and thinking about four little speckled eyes warmed by the breast of its mate,—singing and swinging, and the music in happy waves rippling out of the tiny throat, and the flowers blossoming, the air filled with perfume, and the great white clouds floating in the sky, and the little boy would lean up against the tree and think about Hell and the worm that never dies. Oh! the idea there can be any day too good for a child to be happy in!

Well, after we got over the catechism, then came the sermon in the afternoon, and it was exactly like the one in the fore-noon, except the other end to. Then we started for home—a solemn march—"not a soldier discharged his farewell shot"—and when we got home if we had been real good boys we used to be taken up to the cemetery to cheer us up, and it always did cheer me, those sunken graves, those leaning stones, those gloomy epitaphs covered with the moss of years always cheered me. When I looked at them I said: "Well, this kind of thing can't last always." Then we came back home, and we had books to read which were very eloquent and amusing. We had Josephus, and the "History of the Waldenses," and "Fox's Book of Martyrs," Baxter's "Saint's Rest," and "Jenkyn on the Atonement." I used to read Jenkyn with a good deal of pleasure, and I often thought that the atonement would have to be very broad in its provisions to cover the case of a man that would write such a book for the boys. Then I would look to see how the sun was getting on, and sometimes I thougt it had stuck from pure cussedness. Then I would go back and try Jenkyn's again. Well, but it had to go down, and when the last rim of light sank below the horizon, off would go our hats and we would give three cheers for liberty once again.

I tell you, don't make slaves of your children on Sunday.

The idea that there is any God that hates to hear a child laugh! Let your children play games on Sunday. Here is a poor man that hasn't money enough to go to a big church and he has too much independence to go to a little church that the big church built for charity. He don't want to slide into Heaven that way. I tell you don't come to church, but go to the woods and take your family and a lunch with you, and sit down upon the old log and let the children gather flowers and hear the leaves whispering poems like memories of long ago, and when the sun is about going down, kissing the summits of far hills, go home with your hearts filled with throbs of joy. There is more recreation and joy in that than going to a dry goods box with a steeple on top of it and hearing a man tell you that your chances are about ninety-nine to one for being eternally damned. Let us make this Sunday a day of splendid pleasure, not to excess, but to everything that makes man purer and grander and nobler. I would like to see now something like this: Instead of so many churches, a vast cathedral that would hold twenty or thirty thousand of people, and I would like to see an opera produced in it that would make the souls of men have higher and grander and nobler aims. I would like to see the walls covered with pictures and the niches rich with statuary; I would like to see something put there that you could use in this world now, and I do not believe in sacrificing the present to the future; I do not believe in drinking skimmed milk here with the promise of butter beyond the clouds. Space or time can not be holy any more than a vacuum can be pious. Not a bit, not a bit; and no day can be so holy but what the laugh of a child will make it holier still.

Strike with hand of fire, on, weird musician, thy harp, strung with Apollo's golden hair! Fill the vast cathedral aisles with symphonies sweet and dim, deft toucher of the organ's keys; blow, bugler, blow until thy silver notes do touch and kiss the moonlit waves, and charm the lovers wandering 'mid the vine-clad hills. But know your sweetest strains are discords all compared with childhood's happy laugh—the laugh that fills the eyes with light and every heart with joy! O, rippling river of laughter, thou art the blessed boundary line between the beasts and men, and every wayward wave of thine doth drown some fretful fiend of care. O Laughter, rose lipped daughter of Joy, there are dimples enough in thy cheeks to catch and hold and glorify all the tears of grief.

Don't plant your children in long, straight rows, like posts. Let them have light and air and let them grow beautiful as palms. When I was a little boy children went to bed when they were not sleepy, and always got up when they were. I would like to see that changed, but they say we are too poor, some of us, to do it. Well, all right. It is as easy to wake a child with a kiss as with a blow; with kindness as with a curse, And, another thing; let the children eat what they want to. Let them commence at whichever end of the dinner they desire. That is my doctrine. They know what they want much better than you do. Nature is a great deal smarter than you ever were.

All the advance that has been made in the science of medicine, has been made by the recklessness of patients. I can recollect when they wouldn't give a man water in a fever—not a drop. Now and then some fellow would get so thirsty he would say: " Well, I'll die any way, so I'll drink it," and thereupon he would drink a gallon of water, and thereupon he would burst into a generous perspiration, and get well—

and the next morning when the doctor would come to see him they would tell him about the man drinking the water, and he would say: "How much?"

"Well, he swallowed two pitchers full."

"Is he alive?"

"Yes."

So they would go into the room and the doctor would feel his pulse and ask him:

"Did you drink two pitchers of water?"

"Yes."

"My God! what a constitution you have got."

I tell you there is something splendid in man that will not always mind. Why, if we had done as the kings told us five hundred years ago, we would all have been slaves. If we had done as the priests told us we would all have been idiots. If we had done as the doctors told us we would all have been dead. We have been saved by disobedience. We have been saved by that splendid thing called independence, and I want to see more of it, day after day, and I want to see children raised so they will have it. That is my doctrine. Give the children a chance. Be perfectly honor bright with them, and they will be your friends when you are old. Don't try to teach them something they can never learn. Don't insist upon their pursuing some calling they have no sort of faculty for. Don't make that poor girl play ten years on a piano when she has no ear for music, and when she has practiced until she can play "Bonaparte crossing the Alps," and you can't tell after she has played it whether Bonaparte ever got across or not. Men are oaks, women are vines, children are flowers, and if there is any Heaven in this world, it is in the family. It is where the wife loves the husband, and the husband loves the wife, and where the dimpled arms of children are about the necks of both. That is Heaven, if there is any—and I do not want any better Heaven in another world than that, and if in another world I can not live with the ones I loved here, then I would rather not be there. I would rather resign.

Well, my friends, I have some excuses to make for the race to which I belong. In the first place, this world is not very well adapted to raising good men and good women. It is three times better adapted to the cultivation of fish than of people. There is one little narrow belt running zigag around the world, in which men and women of genius can be raised, and that is all. It is with man as it is with vegetation. In the valley you find the oak and elm tossing their branches defiantly to the storm, and as you advance up the mountain side the hemlock, the pine, the birch, the spruce, the fir, and finally you come to little dwarfed trees, that look like other trees seen through a telescope reversed—every limb twisted as through pain—getting a scanty substance from the miserly crevices of the rocks. You go on and on, until at last the highest crag is freckled with a kind of moss, and vegetation ends. You might as well try to raise oaks and elms where the mosses grow, as to raise great men and great women where their surroundings are unfavorable. You must have the proper climate and soil.

There never has been a man or woman of genius from the southern hemisphere, because the Lord didn't allow the right climate to fall upon the land. It falls upon the water. There never was much civilization except where there has been snow, and ordinarily decent Winter. You can't have civilization without it. Where man needs no bedclothes but clouds, revolution is the normal condition of such a people. It is the Winter that gives us the home; it is the Winter that gives us the fireside and the family relation and all the beautiful flowers of love that adorn that relation. Civilization, liberty, justice, charity and intellectual advancement are all flowers that bloom in the drifted snow. You can't have them anywhere else, and that is the reason we of the north are civilized, and that is the reason that civilization has always been with Winter. That is the reason that philosophy has been here, and, in spite of all our superstitions, we have advanced beyond some of the other races, because we have had this assistance of nature, that drove us into the family relation, that made us prudent; that made us lay up at one time for another season of the year. So there is one excuse I have for my race.

I have got another. I think we came from the lower animals. I am not dead sure of it, but think so. When I first read about it I didn't like it. My heart was filled with sympathy for those people leave nothing to be proud of except ancestors. I thought how terrible this will be upon the nobility of the old world. Think of their being forced to trace their ancestry back to the Duke Orang-Outang or to the Princess Chimpanzee. After thinking it all over I came to the conclusion that I liked that doctrine. I became convinced in spite of myself. I read about rudimentary bones and muscles. I was told that everybody had rudimentary muscles extending from the ear into the cheek. I asked: "What are they?" I was told: "They are the remains of muscles; that they became rudimentary from the lack of use." They went into bankruptcy. They are the muscles with which your ancestors used to flap their ears. Well, at first, I was greatly astonished, and afterward I was more astonished to find they had become rudimentary. How can you account for John Calvin unless we came up from the lower animals? How could you account for a man that would use the extremes of torture unless you admit that there is in man the elements of a snake, of a vulture, a hyena, and a jackal? How can you account for the religious creeds of to-day? How can you account for that infamous doctrine of Hell, except with an animal origin? How can you account for your conception of a God that would sell women and babes into slavery?

Well, I thought that thing over and I began to like it after a while, and I said: "It is not so much difference who my father was as who his son is." And I finally said I would rather belong to a race that commenced with the skulless vertebrates in the dim Laurentian seas, that wriggled without knowing why they wriggled, swimming without knowing where they were going, that come along up by degrees through millions of ages, through all that crawls, and swims, and floats, and runs, and growls, and barks, and howls, until it struck this fellow in the dug-out. And then that fellow in the dug-out getting a little grander, and each one below calling every one above him a heretic, calling every one who had made a little advance an infidel or an atheist, and finally the heads getting a little higher and donning up a little grander and more splendidly, and finally produced Shakspeare, who harvested all the field of dramatic thought and from whose day until now there have been none but gleaners of chaff and straw. Shakspeare was an intellectual ocean whose waves touched all the shores of human thought, within which were all the tides and currents and pulses upon which lay all the lights and shadows, and over which brooded all the calms, and swept all the storms and tempests of which the soul is capable. I would rather belong to that race that commenced with that skulless vertebrate; that produced Shakspeare, a race that has before it an infinite future, with the angel of progress leaning from the far horizon, beckoning men forward and upward forever. I would rather belong to that race than to have descended from a perfect pair upon which the Lord has lost money every moment from that day to this.

Now, my crime has been this: I have insisted that the Bible is not the word of God. I have insisted that we should not whip our children. I have insisted that we should treat our wives as loving equals. I have denied that God—if there is any God—ever upheld polygamy and slavery. I have denied that that God ever told his generals to kill innocent babes and tear and rip open women with the sword of war. I have denied that, and for that I have been assailed by the clergy of the United States. They tell me I have misquoted; and I owe it to you, and maybe I owe it to myself, to read one or two words to you upon this subject. In order to do that I shall have to put on my glasses; and that brings me back to where I started—that man has advanced just in proportion as his thought has mingled with his labor. If man's eyes hadn't failed he would never have made any spectacles, he would never have had the telescope, and he never would have been able to read the leaves of Heaven.

Mr. Ingersoll's Reply to Dr. Collyer.

Now, they tell me—and there are several gentlemen who have spoken on this subject—the Rev. Mr. Collyer, a gentleman standing as high as anybody, and I have nothing to say against him, because I denounce a God who upheld murder, and slavery and polygamy, he says that what I said was slang. I would like to have it compared with any sermon that ever issued from the lips of that gentleman. And before he gets through he admits that the Old Testament is a rotten tree that will soon fall into the earth and act as a fertilizer for his doctrine.

Is it honest in that man to assail my motive? Let him answer my argument! Is it honest and fair in him to say I am doing a certain thing because it is popular? Has it got to this, that, in this Christian country, where they have preached every day hundreds and thousands of sermons—has it got to this that infidelity is so popular in the United States?

If it has, I take courage. And I not only see the dawn of a brighter day, but the day is here. Think of it! A minister tells me in this year of grace, 1879, that a man is an infidel simply that he may be popular. I am glad of it. Simply that he may make money. Is it possible that we can make more money tearing up churches than in building them up? Is it possible that we can make more money denouncing the God of slavery than we can praising the God that took liberty from man? If so, I am glad.

I call publicly upon Robert Collyer—a man for whom I have great respect—I call publicly upon Robert Collyer to state to the people of this city whether he believes the Old Testament was inspired. I call upon him to state whether he believes that God ever upheld these institutions; whether he believes that God was a polygamist; whether he believes that God commanded Moses or Joshua or any one else to slay little children in the cradle. Do you believe that Robert Collyer would obey such an order? Do you believe that he would rush to the cradle and drive the knife of theological hatred to the tender heart of a dimpled child? And yet when I denounce a God that will give such a hellish order, he says it is slang.

I want him to answer; and when he answers he will say he does not believe the Bible is inspired. That is what he will say, and he holds these old worthies in the same contempt that I do. Suppose he should act like Abraham. Suppose he should send some woman out into the wilderness with his child in her arms to starve, would he think that mankind ought to hold his name up forever, for reverence?

Robert Collyer says that we should read and scan every word of the Old Testament with reverence; that we should take this book up with reverential hands. I deny it. We should read it as we do every other book, and everything good in it, keep it; and everything that shocks the brain and shocks the heart, throw it away. Let us be honest.

Mr. Ingersoll's Reply to Prof. Swing.

Prof. Swing has made a few remarks on this subject, and I say the spirit he has exhibited has been as gentle and as sweet as the perfume of a flower. He was too good a man to stay in the Presbyterian church. He was a rose among thistles. He was a dove among vultures—and they hunted him out, and I am glad he came out. I tell all the churches to drive all such men out, and when he comes I want him to state just what he thinks. I want him to tell the people of Chicago whether he believes the Bible is inspired in any sense except that in which Shakspeare was inspired. Honor bright I tell you that all the sweet and beautiful things in the Bible would not make one play of Shakspeare, all the philosophy in the world would not make one scene in Hamlet, all the beauties of the Bible would not make one scene in the Midsummer Night's Dream; all the beautiful things about woman in the Bible would not begin to create such a character as Perdita or Imogene or Miranda. Not one.

I want him to tell whether he believes the Bible was inspired in any other way than Shakspeare was inspired. I want him to pick out something as beautiful and tender as Burns' poem to Mary in Heaven. I want him to tell whether he believes the story about the bears eating up children; whether that is inspired. I want him to tell whether he considers that a poem or not. I want to know if the same God made those bears that devoured the children because they laughed at an old man out of hair. I want to know if the same God that did that is the same God who said, "Suffer little children to come unto me, for such is the kingdom of Heaven." I want him to answer it, and answer it fairly. That is all I ask. I want just the fair thing.

Now, sometimes Mr. Swing talks as though he believed the Bible, and then he talks to me as though he didn't believe the Bible. The day he made this sermon I think he did, just a little, believe it. He is like the man that passed a ten dollar counterfeit bill. He was arrested, and his father went to see him and said, "John, how could you commit such a crime? How could you bring my gray hairs in sorrow to the grave?" "Well," he says, "father, I'll tell you. I got this bill and some days I thought it was bad and some days I thought it was good, and one day when I thought it was good I passed it."

I want it distinctly understood that I have the greatest respect for Prof. Swing, but I want him to tell whether the 109th psalm is inspired.

I want him to tell whether the passages I shall afterward read in this book are inspired. That is what I want.

Ingersoll's Reply to Brooke Herford, D.D.

Then there is another gentleman here. His name is Herford. He says it is not fair to apply the test of truth to the Bible—I don't think it is myself. He says although Moses upheld slavery, that he improved it. They were not quite as bad as they were before, and Heaven justified slavery at that time. Do you believe that God ever turned the arms of children into chains of slavery? Do you believe that God ever said to a man: "You can't have your wife unless you will be a slave! You can not have your children unless you will lose your liberty; and unless you are willing to throw them from your heart forever, you can not be free?" I want Mr. Herford to state whether he loves such a God. Be honor bright about it. Don't begin to talk about civilization, or what the church has done or will do. Just walk right up to the rack and say whether you love and worship a God that established slavery. Honest! And love and worship a God that would allow a little babe to be torn from the breast of its mother and sold into slavery. Now tell it fair, Mr. Herford, I want you to tell the ladies in your congregation that you believe in a God that allowed women to be given to the soldiers. Tell them that, and then if you say it was not the God of Moses, then don't praise Moses any more. Don't do it. Answer these questions.

The Ingersoll Gattling Gun Turned on Dr. Ryder.

Then here is another gentleman, Mr. Ryder, the Rev. Mr. Ryder, and he says that Calvinism is rejected by a majority of Christendom. He is mistaken. There is what they call the Evangelical Alliance. They met in this country in 1875 or 1876, and there were present representatives of all the evangelical churches in the world, and they adopted a creed, and that creed is that man is totally depraved. That creed is that there is an eternal, universal Hell, and that every man that does not believe in a certain way is bound to be damned forever, and that there is only one way to be saved, and that is by faith, and by faith alone; and they would not allow anybody to be represented there that did not believe that, and they would not allow a Unitarian there, and would not have allowed Dr. Ryder there, because he takes away from the Christian world the consolation naturally arising from the belief in Hell.

Dr. Ryder is mistaken. All the orthodox religion of the day is Calvinism. It believes in the fall of man. It believes in the atonement. It believes in the eternity of Hell, and it believes in salvation by faith; that is to say, by credulity.

That is what they believe, and he is mistaken; and I want to tell Dr. Ryder to-day, if there is a God, and He wrote the Old Testament, there is a Hell. The God that wrote the Old Testament will have a Hell. And I want to tell Dr. Ryder another thing, that the Bible teaches an eternity of punishment. want to tell him that the Bible upholds the doctrine of Hell. I want to tell him that if there is no Hell, somebody ought to have said so, and Jesus Christ himself should not have said: "I will at the last day say: 'Depart from me, ye cursed, into everlasting fire prepared for the devil and his angels.'" If there was not such a place, Christ would not have said: "Depart from me, ye cursed, and these shall go hence into everlasting fire." And if you, Dr. Ryder, are depending for salvation on the God that wrote the Old Testament, you will inevitably be eternally damned.

There is no hope for you. It is just as bad to deny Hell as it is to deny Heaven. It is just as much blasphemy to deny the devil as to deny God, according to the orthodox creed. He admits that the Jews were polygamists, but, he says, how was it they finally quit it? I can tell you—the soil was so poor they couldn't afford it. Prof. Swing says the Bible is a poem. Dr. Ryder says it is a picture. The Garden of Eden is pictorial; a pictorial snake and a pictorial woman, I suppose, and a pictorial man, and maybe it was a pictorial sin. And only a pictorial atonement.

Ingersoll's Reply to Rabbi Bien.

Then there is another gentleman, and he a rabbi, a Rabbi Bien, or Bean, or whatever his name is, and he comes to the defense of the Great Law-giver. There was another rabbi who attacked me in Cincinnati, and I couldn't help but think of the old saying, that a man got off when he said the tallest man he ever knew, his name was Short. And the fattest man he ever saw, his name was Lean. And it is only necessary for me to add that this rabbi in Cincinnati was Wise.

The rabbi here, I will not answer him, and I will tell you why. Because he has taken himself outside of all the limits of a gentleman; because he has taken it upon himself to traduce American women in language the beastliest I ever read; and any man who says that the American women are not just as good women as any God can make, and pick his mud to-day, is an unappreciative barbarian.

I will let him alone because he denounced all the men in this country, all the members of Congress, all the members of the Senate, and all the judges upon the Bench; in his lecture he denounced them as thieves and robbers. That won't do. I want to remind him that in this country the Jews were first admitted to the privileges of citizens; that in this country they were first given all their rights, and I am as much in favor of their having their rights as I am in favor of having my own. But when a rabbi so far forgets himself as to traduce the women and men of this country, I pronounce him a vulgar falsifier, and let him alone.

Strange, that nearly every man that has answered me, has answered me mostly on the same side. Strange, that nearly every man that thought himself called upon to defend the Bible was one who did not believe in it himself. Isn't it strange? They are like some suspected people, always anxious to show their marriage certificate. They want at least to convince the world that they are not as bad as I am.

Now, I want to read you just one or two things, and then I am going to let you go. I want to see if I have said such awful things, and whether I have got any scripture to stand by me. I will only read two or three verses. Does the Bible teach man to enslave his brother? If it does, it is not the word of God, unless God is a slaveholder.

Moreover, all the children of the strangers that do sojourn among you, of them shall ye buy of their families which are with you, which they beget in your land, and they shall be your possession. Ye shall take them as an inheritance for your children after you to inherit them. They shall be your bondsmen forever. (Old Testament.)

Upon the limbs of unborn babes this fiendish God put the chains of slavery. I hate him.

Both thy bondmen and bondwomen shall be of the heathen round about thee, and them shall ye buy, bondmen and bondwomen.

Now let us read what the New Testament has. I could read a great deal more, but that is enough.

Servants, be obedient to them that are your masters, according to the flesh in fear and trembling, in singleness of your heart, as unto Christ.

This is putting the dirty thief that steals your labor on an equality with God.

Servants, be subject to your masters with all fear; not only to the good and gentle but also to the froward.

For this is thankworthy, if a man for conscience toward God endure grief, suffering wrongfully.

The idea of a man on account of conscience toward God stealing another man, or allowing him nothing but lashes on his back as legal-tender for labor performed.

Let as many servants as are under the yoke count their own masters worthy of all honor, that the name of God and His doctrine be not blasphemed.

How can you blaspheme the name of God by asserting your independence? How can you blaspheme the name of a God by striking fetters from the limbs of men? I wish some of your answers would tell me that. "And they that have believing masters let them not despise them." That is to say, a good Christian could own another believer in Jesus Christ; could own a woman and her children, and could sell the child away from its mother. That is a sweet belief. O, hypocrisy!

Let them not despise them because they are brethren, but rather do them service because they are faithful and beloved, partakers of the benefit.

Oh, what slush! Here is what they tell the poor slave, so that he will serve the man that stole his wife and children from him:

For we brought nothing into this world, and it is certain we can carry nothing out. Having food and raiment let us be therewith content.

Don't you think that it would do just as well to preach that to the thieving man as to the suffering slave? I think so. Then this same Bible teaches witchcraft, that spirits go into the bodies of the man, and pigs; and that God himself made a trade with the devil, and the devil traded him off—a man for a certain number of swine, and the devil lost money because the hogs ran right down into the sea. He got a corner on that deal.

Now let us see how they believed in the rights of children:

If a man have a stubborn and a rebellious son which will not obey the voice of his father, or the voice of his mother, and that, when they have chastened him, will not harken unto them, then shall his father and his mother lay hold on him, and bring him out unto the elders of his city, and unto the gate of his place. And they shall say unto the elders of his city, This, our son, is stubborn and rebellious, he will not obey our voice, he is a glutton and a drunkard. And all the men of his city shall stone him with stones, that he die, so shalt thou put evil away.

That is a very good way to raise children. Here is the story of Jephthah. He went off and he asked the Lord to let him whip some people, and he told the Lord if He would let him whip them, he would sacrifice to the Lord the first thing that met him on his return; and the first thing that met him was his own beautiful daughter, and he sacrificed her. Is there a sadder story in all the history of the world than that? What do you think of a man that would sacrifice his own daughter? What do you think of a God that would receive that sacrifice? Now, then, they come to women in this blessed gospel, and let us see what the gospel says about women. Then you ought all to go to church, girls, next Sunday and hear it. "Let the woman learn in silence with all subjection; suffer not woman to think nor usurp authority over man, for Adam was formed first, not Eve."

Don't you see?

"Adam was not deceived, but the woman being deceived was in the transgession. Notwithstanding all this she shall be saved in childbearing if she continues in faith and charity and holiness with sobriety." (That is Mr. Timothy.) "But I would have you know that the head of every man is Christ, and the head of the woman is the man, and the head of Christ is God."

I suppose that every old maid is acephalous.

"For a man indeed ought not to cover head, forasmuch as he is the image and glory of God; but the woman is the glory of man. For the man is not of the woman, but woman of the man. Neither was the man created for the woman, but the woman for the man. Wives, submit yourselves unto your own husband as unto the Lord, for the husband is the head of the wife even as Christ is the head of the Church."

Do you hear that! You didn't know how much we were above you. When you go back to the Old Testament, to the great law-giver, you find that the woman has to ask forgiveness for having borne a child. If it was a boy, thirty-three days she was unclean; if it was a girl sixty-six. Nice laws! Good laws! If there is a pure thing in this world, if there is a picture of perfect purity, it is a mother with her child in her arms. Yes, I think more of a good woman and a child than I do of all the gods I have ever heard these people tell about. Just think of this:

When thou goest forth to war against thine enemies, and the Lord thy God hath delivered them into thine hands, and thou hast taken them captive, and seest among the captive a beautiful woman and hast a desire unto her that thou wouldst have her to thy wife, then thou shalt bring her home to thine house, and she shall shave her head, and pare her nails.

Wherefore, ye must needs be subject not only for love, but for conscience sake, and for this cause pay ye tribute, for they are God's ministers.

I despise this wretched doctrine. Wherever the sword of rebellion is drawn in favor of the right, I am a rebel. I suppose Alexander, czar of Russia, was put there by the order of God, was he? I am sorry he was not removed by the nihilist that shot at him the other day.

I tell you in a country like that, where there are hundreds of girls not 16 years of age prisoners in Siberia, simply for giving their ideas about liberty, and we telegraphed to that country congratulating that wretch that he was not killed, my heart goes into the prison, my heart goes with the poor girl working as a miner in the mines, crawling on her hands and knees getting the precious ore out of the mines, and my sympathies go with her, and my sympathies cluster around the point of the dagger.

Does the Bible describe a God of mercy? Let me read you a verse or two.

I will make my arrows drunk with blood, and my sword shall devour flesh. Thy foot may be dipped in the blood of thine enemies.

And the tongue of thy dogs in the same.

And the Lord thy God will put out those nations before thee by little and little; thou mayest not consume them at once, lest the beasts of the field increase upon thee.

But the Lord thy God shall deliver them unto thee, and shall destroy them with a mighty destruction, until they be destroyed.

And He shall deliver their kings unto thine hand, and thou shalt destroy their name from under Heaven; then shall no man be able to stand before thee, until thou have destroyed them.

I can see what he had her nails pared for. Does the Bible teach polygamy?

The Rev. Dr. Newman, consul general to all the world—had a discussion with Elder Heber or Kimball, or some such wretch in Utah—

whether the Bible sustains polygamy, and the Mormons have printed that discussion as a campaign document. Read the order of Moses in the 31st chapter of Numbers. A great many chapters I dare not read to you. They are too filthy. I leave all that to the clergy. Read the 31st chapter of Exodus, the 31st chapter of Deuteronomy, the life of Abraham, and the life of David, and the life of Solomon, and then tell me that the Bible does not uphold polygamy and concubinage!

Let them answer. Then I said that the Bible upheld tyranny. Let me read you a little: "Let every soul be subject to the higher powers—the powers that be are ordained of God."

George III. was king by the grace of God, and when our fathers rose in rebellion, according to this doctrine, they rose against the power of God; and if they did they were successful.

And so it goes on telling of all the cities that were destroyed, and of the great-hearted men, that they dashed their brains out, and all the little babes, and all the sweet women that they killed and plundered—all in the name of a most merciful God. Well, think of it! The Old Testament is filled with anathemas, and with curses, and with words of revenge, and jealousy, and hatred, and meanness, and brutality.

Have I read enough to show that what I said is so? I think I have. I wish I had time to read to you further of what the dear old fathers of the church said about woman—wait a minute, and I will read you a little. We have got them running.

St. Augustine in his 22d book says: "A woman ought to serve her husband as unto God, affirming that woman ought to be braced and bridled betimes, if she aspire to any dominion, alleging that dangerous and perilous it is to suffer her to precede, although it be in temporal and corporeal things. How can woman be in the image of God, seeing she is subject to man, and hath no authority to teach, neither to be a witness, neither to judge, much less to rule or bear the rod of empire."

Oh, he is a good one. These are the very words of Augustine. Let me read some more. "Woman shall be subject unto man as unto Christ." That is St. Augustine, and this sentence of Augustine ought to be noted of all women, for in it he plainly affirms that women are all the more subject to man. And now, St. Ambrose, he is a good boy. "Adam was deceived by Eve—called Heva—and not Heva by Adam, and therefore just it is that woman receive and acknowledge him for governor whom she called sin, lest that again she slip and fall with womanly facility." Don't you see that woman has sinned once, and man never? If you give woman an opportunity, she will sin again, whereas if you give it to man, who never, never, never betrayed his trust in the world, nothing bad can happen. "Let women be subject to their own husbands as unto the Lord, for man is the head of woman, and Christ is the head of the congregation." They are all real good men, all of them. "It is not permitted to woman to speak; let her be in silence; as the law said: unto thy husband shalt thou ever be, and he shall bear dominion over thee."

So St. Chrysostom. He is another good man. "Woman," he says, "was put under the power of man, and man was pronounced lord over her; that she should obey man, that the head should not follow the feet. False priests do commonly deceive women, because they are easily persuaded to any opinion, especially if it be again given, and because they lack prudence and right reason to judge the things that be spoken; which should not be the nature of those that are appointed to govern others. For they should be constant, stable, prudent, and doing everything with discretion and reason: which virtues woman can not have in equality with man."

I tell you women are more prudent than men. I tell you, as a rule, women are more truthful then men. I tell you that women are more faithful than men—ten times as faithful as man. I never saw a man pursue his wife into the very ditch and dust of degradation and take her in his arms. I never saw a man stand at the shore where she had been morally wrecked, waiting for the waves to bring back even her corpse to his arms; but I have seen woman do it. I have seen woman with her white arms lift man from the mire of degradation, and hold him to her bosom as though he were an angel.

And these men thought woman not fit to be held as pure in the sight of God as man. I never saw a man that pretended that he didn't love a woman; that pretended that he loved God better than he did a woman, that he didn't look hateful to me, hateful and unclean. I could read you twenty others, but I haven't time to do it. They are all to the same effect exactly. They hate woman, and say man is as much above her as God is above man. I am a believer in absolute equality. I am a believer in absolute liberty between man and wife. I believe in liberty, and I say, "Oh, liberty, float not forever in the far horizon—remain not forever in the dream of the enthusiast, the philanthropist and poet; bu come and make thy home among the children of men."

I know not what discoveries, what inventions, what thoughts may leap from the brain of the world. I know not what garments of glory may be woven by the years to come. I can not dream of the victories to be won upon the field of thought; but I do know that, coming down the infinite sea of the future, there will never touch this "bank and shoal of time" a richer gift, a rarer blessing than liberty for man, woman and child.

I never addressed a more magnificent audience in my life, and I thank you, I thank you a thousand times over.

Ingersoll's Catechism and Bible Class.

Nothing is more gratifying than to see ideas that were received with scorn, flourishing in the sunshine of approval. Only a few weeks ago I stated that the Bible was not inspired; that Moses was mistaken, that the "flood" was a foolish myth; that the Tower of Babel existed only in credulity; that God did not create the universe from nothing, that He did not start the first woman with a rib; that He never upheld slavery; that He was not a polygamist; that He did not kill people for making hair-oil: that He did not order His Generals to kill the dimpled babes; that He did not allow the roses of love and the violets of modesty to be trodden under the brutal feet of lust; that the Hebrew language was written without vowels; that the Bible was composed of many books written by unknown men; that all translations differed from each other, and that this book had filled the world with agony and crime.

At that time I had not the remotest idea that the most learned clergymen in Chicago would substantially agree with me—in public. I have read the replies of the Rev. Robert Collyer, Dr. Thomas, Rabbi Kohler, Rev. Brooke Herford, Prof Swing, and Dr. Ryder, and will now ask them a few questions, answering them in their own words:

First, Rev. ROBERT COLLYER: Question. What is your opinion of the Bible? Answer. "It is a splendid book. It makes the noblest type of Catholics and the meanest bigots. Through this book men give their hearts for good to God, or for evil to the Devil. The best argument for the intrinsic greatness of the book is that it can touch such wide extremes, and seem to maintain us in the most unparalleled cruelty, as well as the most tender mercy; that it can inspire purity like that of the great saints and afford arguments in favor of polygamy. The Bible is the text book of ironclad Calvinism and sunny Universalism. It makes the Quaker quiet and the Millerite crazy. It inspired the Union soldier to live and grandly die for the right, and Stonewall Jackson to live nobly and die grandly for the wrong."

Q. But, Mr. Collyer, do you really think that a book with as many passages in favor of wrong as right, is inspired? A. "I look upon the Old Testament as a rotting tree. When it falls it will fertilize a bank of violets."

Q. Do you believe that God upheld slavery and polygamy? Do you believe that He ordered the killing of babes and the violation of maidens? A. "There is three-fold inspiration in the Bible, the first peerless and perfect, the Word of God to man; the second simply and purely human, and then below this again, there is an inspiration born of an evil heart, ruthless and savage there and then as anything well can be. A three-fold inspiration, of Heaven first, then of the Earth, and then of Hell, all in the same book, all sometimes in the same chapter, and then, besides, a great many things that need no inspiration."

Q. Then, after all, you do not pretend that the Scriptures are really inspired? A. "The Scriptures make no such claim for themselves as the Church makes for them. They leave me free to say this is false, or this is true. The truth even within the Bible dies and lives, makes on this side and loses on that."

Q. What do you say to the last verse in the Bible, where a curse is threatened to any man who takes from or adds to the book? A. "I have but one answer to this question, and it is: Let who will have written this, I can not for an instant believe that it was written by a divine inspiration. Such dogmas and threats as these are not of God, but of man, and not of any man of a free spirit and heart eager for the truth, but a narrow man who would cripple and confine the human soul in its quest after the whole truth of God, and back those who have done the shameful things in the name of the Most High."

Q. Do you not regard such talk as "slang?"

(Supposed) Answer. If an infidel had said that the writer of Revelations was narrow and bigoted, I might have denounced his discourse as "slang," but I think that Unitarian ministers can do so with the greatest propriety.

Q. Do you believe in the stories of the Bible, about Jael, and the sun standing still, and the walls falling at the blowing of horns? A. "They may be legends, myths, poems, or what they will, but they are not the Word of God. So I say again, it was not the God and Father of us all who inspired the woman to drive that nail crashing through the king's temple after she had given him that bowl of milk and bid him sleep in safety, but a very mean Devil of hatred and revenge that I should hardly expect to find in a squaw on the plains. It was not the ram's horns and the shouting before which the walls fell flat. If they went down at all, it was through good solid pounding. And not for an instant did the steady sun stand still or let his planet stand still while barbarian fought barbarian. He kept just the time then he keeps now. They might believe it who made the record. I do not. And since the whole Christian world might believe it, still we do not who gather in this church. A free and reasonable mind stands right in our way. Newton might believe it as a Christian and disbelieve it as a philosopher. We stand then with the philosopher against the Christian, for we must believe what is true to us in the last test, and these things are not true."

SECOND, REV. DR. THOMAS. Question. What is your opinion of the Old Testament? Answer. "My opinion is that it is not one book, but many—thirty-nine books bound up in one. The date and authorship of most of these books are wholly unknown. The Hebrews wrote without vowels and without dividing the letters into syllables, words or sentences. The books were gathered up by Ezra. At that time only two of the Jewish tribes remained. All progress had ceased. In gathering up the sacred book, copyists exercised great liberty in making changes and additions."

Q. Yes, we know all that, but is the Old Testament inspired? A. "There may be the inspiration of art, of poetry, or oratory; of patriotism—and there are such inspirations. There are moments when great truths and principles come to men. They seek the man and not the man them."

Q. Yes, we all admit that, but is the Bible inspired? A. "But still I know of no way to convince any one of spirit and inspiration and God only as His reason may take hold of these things."

Q. Do you think the Old Testament true? A. "The story of Eden may be an allegory; the history of the children of Israel may have mistakes."

Q. Must inspiration claim infallibility? A. "It is a mistake to say that if you believe one part of the Bible you must believe all. Some of the thirty-nine books may be inspired, others not; or there may be degrees of inspiration."

Q. Do you believe that God commanded the soldiers to kill the children and the married women and save for themselves the maidens, as recorded in Numbers 31:2? Do you believe that God upheld slavery? Do you believe that God upheld polygamy? A. "The Bible may be wrong in some statements. God and right can not be wrong. We must not exalt the Bible above God. It may be that we have claimed too much for the Bible, and thereby given not a little occasion for such men as Mr. Ingersoll to appear at the other extreme, denying too much."

Q. What then shall be done? A. "We must take a middle ground. It is not necessary to believe that the bears devoured the forty-two children, nor that Jonah was swallowed by the whale."

THIRD, REV. DR. KOHLER. Question. What is your opinion about the Old Testament? Answer. "I will not make futile attempts of artificially interpreting the letter of the Bible so as to make it reflect the philosophical, moral and scientific views of our time. The Bible is a sacred record of humanity's childhood."

Q. Are you an orthodox Christian? A. "No. Orthodoxy, with its face turned backward to a ruined temple or a dead Messiah, is fast becoming like Lot's wife, a pillar of salt."

Q. Do you really believe the Old Testament was inspired? A. "I greatly acknowledge our indebtedness to men like Voltaire and Thomas Paine, whose bold denial and cutting wit were so instrumental in bringing about this glorious era of freedom, so congenial and blissful, particularly to the long-abused Jewish race."

Q. Do you believe in the inspiration of the Bible? A. "Of course there is a destructive axe needed to strike down the old building in order to make room for the grander new. The divine origin claimed by the Hebrews for their national literature was claimed by all nations for their old records and laws as preserved by the priesthood. As Moses, the Hebrew law-giver, is represented as having received the law from God on the holy mountain, so is Zoroaster, the Persian, Manu, the Hindoo, Minos, the Cretan, Lycurgus, the Spartan, and Numa, the Roman."

Q. Do you believe all the stories in the Bible? A. "All that can and must be said against them is that they have been too long retained around the arms and limbs of grown-up manhood to check the spiritual progress of religion; that by Jewish ritualism and Christian dogmatism they became fetters unto the soul, turning the light of Heaven into a misty haze to blind the eye, and even into a Hell fire of fanaticism to consume souls."

Q. Is the Bible inspired? A. "True, the Bible is not free from errors, nor is any work of man and time. It abounds in childish views and offensive matters. I trust that it will, in a time not far off, be presented for common use in families, schools, synagogues and churches, in a refined shape, cleansed from all dross and chaff, and stumbling-blocks on which the scoffer delights to dwell."

FOURTH, REV. MR. HERFORD. Question. Is the Bible true? Answer. "Ingersoll is very fond of saying 'The question is not, is the Bible inspired, but is it true?' That sounds very plausible, but you know as applied to any ancient book it is simply nonsense."

Q. Do you think the stories in the Bible exaggerated? A. "I dare say the numbers are immensely exaggerated."

Q. Do you think that God upheld polygamy? A. "The truth of which simply is, that four thousand years ago polygamy existed among the Jews, as everywhere else on earth then, and even their prophets did not come to the idea of its being wrong. But what is there to be indignant about in that?"

Q. And so you really wonder why any man should be indignant at the idea that God upheld and sanctioned that beastliness called polygamy? A. "What is there to be indignant about in that?"

FIFTH, PROF. SWING. Question. What is your idea of the Bible? Answer. "I think it a poem."

SIXTH, REV. DR. RYDER. Question. And what is your idea of the sacred Scriptures? Answer. "Like other nations, the Hebrews had their patriotic, descriptive, didactic and lyrical poems in the same varieties as other nations; but with them, unlike other nations, whatever may be the form of their poetry, it always possesses the characteristic of religion."

Q. I suppose you fully appreciate the religious characteristics of the Song of Solomon? No answer.

Q. Does the Bible uphold polygamy? A. "The law of Moses did not forbid it, but contained many provisions against its worst abuses, and such as were intended to restrict it within narrow limits."

Q. So you think God corrected some of the worst abuses of polygamy, but preserved the institution itself?

I might question many others, but have concluded not to consider those as members of my Bible class who deal in calumnies and epithets. From the so-called "replies" of such ministers it appears that, while Christianity changes the heart, it does not improve the manners, and that one can get into Heaven in the next world without having been a gentleman in this.

It is difficult for me to express the deep and thrilling satisfaction I have experienced in reading the admissions of the clergy of Chicago. Surely the battle of intellectual liberty is almost won when ministers admit that the Bible is filled with ignorant and cruel mistakes; that each man has the right to think for himself, and that it is not necessary to believe the Scriptures in order to be saved.

From the bottom of my heart I congratulate my pupils on the advance they have made, and hope soon to meet them on the serene heights of perfect freedom.

INGERSOLL AT HIS BROTHER'S GRAVE

The funeral of Hon. Ebon C. Ingersoll, brother of Col. Robert G. Ingersoll, of Illinois, took place at his residence in Washington, D. C., June 2, 1879. The ceremonies were extremely simple, consisting merely of viewing the remains by relatives and friends, and a funeral oration by Col. Robert G. Ingersoll, brother of the deceased. A large number of distinguished gentlemen were present, including Secretary Sherman, Assistant Secretary Hawley, Senators Blaine, Voorhees, Paddock, Allison, Logan, Hon. Thomas Henderson, Gov. Pound, Hon. Wm. M. Morrison, Gen. Jeffreys, Gen. Williams, Col. James Fishback, and others. The pall-bearers were Senators Blaine, Voorhees, David Davis, Paddock and Allison, Col. Ward, H. Lamon, Hon. Jeremiah Wilson of Indiana, and Hon. Thomas A. Boyd of Illinois.

Soon after Mr. Ingersoll began to read his eloquent characterization of the dead, his eyes filled with tears. He tried to hide them behind his eye-glasses, but he could not do it, and finally he bowed his head upon the dead man's coffin in uncontrolable grief. It was after some delay and the greatest efforts at self-mastery, that Col. Ingersoll was able to finish reading his address, which was as follows:

Colonel Ingersoll's Funeral Oration.

MY FRIENDS: I am going to do that which the dead often promised he would do for me. The loved and loving brother, husband, father, friend, died where manhood's morning almost touches noon, and while the shadows still were falling toward the West. He had not passed on life's highway the stone that marks the highest point, but being weary for a moment he laid down by the wayside, and, using his burden for a pillow, fell into that dreamless sleep that kisses down his eyelids still. While yet in love with life and raptured with the world, he passed to silence and pathetic dust. Yet, after all, it may be best, just in the happiest, sunniest hour of all the voyage, while eager winds are kissing every sail, to dash against the unseen rock, and in an instant hear the billows roar a sunken ship. For, whether in mid-sea or among the breakers of the farther shore, a wreck must mark at last the end of each and all. And every life, no matter if its every hour is rich with love and every moment jeweled with a joy, will, at its close, become a tragedy, as sad, and deep, and dark as can be woven of the warp and woof of mystery and death. This brave and tender man in every storm of life was oak and rock, but in the sunshine he was vine and flower. He was the friend of all heroic souls. He climbed the heights and left all superstitions far below, while on his forehead fell the golden dawning of a grander day. He loved the beautiful and was with color, form and music touched to tears. He sided with the weak, and with a willing hand gave alms; with loyal heart and with the purest hand he faithfully discharged all public trusts. He was a worshipper of liberty and a friend of the oppressed. A thousand times I have heard him quote the words: "For justice all place a temple and all season summer." He believed that happiness was the only good, reason the only torch, justice the only worshipper, humanity the only religion, and love the priest.

He added to the sum of human joy, and were every one for whom he did some loving service to bring a blossom to his grave he would sleep to-night beneath a wilderness of flowers. Life is a narrow vale between the cold and barren peaks of two eternities. We strive in vain to look beyond the heights. We cry aloud, and the only answer is the echo of our wailing cry. From the voiceless lips of the unreplying dead there comes no word; but in the night of death hope sees a star and listening love can hear the rustle of a wing. He who sleeps here, when dying, mistaking the approach of death for the return of health, whispered with his latest breath, "I am better now." Let us believe, in spite of doubts and dogmas and tears and fears that these dear words are true of all the countless dead. And now, to you who have been chosen from among the many men he loved to do the last sad office for the dead, we give his sacred dust. Speech can not contain our love. There was—there is—no gentler, stronger, manlier man.

POPULAR BOOKS PUBLISHED BY RHODES & McCLURE,
CHICAGO.

TWENTIETH THOUSAND.

MISTAKES of INGERSOLL
(No. 1,)

AS SHOWN BY

Prof. Swing; W. H. Ryder, D.D.; Brooke Herford, D.D.; J. Monro Gibson, D.D.; Rabbi Wise, and Others,

Including also Mr. Ingersoll's Lecture, entitled

"THE MISTAKES OF MOSES."

8vo., 128 Pages.   Edited by J. B. McCLURE.

Price in Paper Cover, 35 Cents.   Sent by Mail, post paid, on receipt of price, by the publishers.

"The collection is timely and creditable, and its fairness in presenting both the text and comments is commendable."—*Chicago Evening Journal.*

"An interesting book; it is not often that a public character like this famous lecturer is subjected to criticism, which is at once so fair and so acute, so civil in manner, and yet so just, as in these instances."—*Advance.*

INGERSOLL'S ANSWERS
TO

Prof. Swing; W. H. Ryder, D.D.; Dr. Thomas; Dr. Collyer; Brooke Herford, D.D.; Dr. Koehler; and

INGERSOLL'S LECTURE ON "SKULLS"

INCLUDING ALSO

MISTAKES OF INGERSOLL
(No. 2.)

AS SHOWN BY

Bishop Cheney; Chaplain McCabe; Rev. W. F. Crafts; Robert Collyer, D.D.; Arthur Swazey, D.D.; Fred. Perry Powers, and others.

8vo., 150 Pages.   Edited by J. B. McClure.   Price in Paper Cover, 35 Cents.
Sent by mail, post paid, on receipt of price, by the publishers.

"MISTAKES OF INGERSOLL,"
AND
"INGERSOLL'S ANSWERS."

8 vo., 270 pages. Including full contents of No. 1 and No. 2 (two volumes in one), bound in cloth; fine. Price, $1.00. Sent by mail, post paid, on receipt of price, by the publishers.

RHODES & McCLURE, Publishers,
1879.   Methodist Church Block, Chicago.

POPULAR BOOKS PUBLISHED BY RHODES & McCLURE
CHICAGO.

TENTH THOUSAND.

"EDISON AND HIS INVENTIONS."

8 vo., 178 pages. Illustrated.

EDITED BY J. B. McCLURE.

Price in Cloth, fine, $1.00, Paper Covers, 50 cts.

This book contains the many interesting incidents, and all the essential facts, connected with the life of the great inventor, together with a full explanation of his principal inventions, including the phonograph, telephone, and electric light, which are explained by the aid of diagrams.

OPINIONS OF THE PRESS.

"*Edison and His Inventions*" is one of the latest and most entertaining books that has been laid on our table. A glance at the title-page assures us that the book cannot fail to be interesting when we see that it has been compiled by Mr. J. B. McClure, of the well known firm of Rhodes & McClure. Mr. McClure has spent months in correspondence with parties who were acquainted with Edison in his boyhood days, and also with the parents of the great inventor, who have furnished numerous amusing anecdotes which have not as yet been made public. The tasimeter, phonograph, telephone, and all his inventions, are illustrated, and the details explained in such a manner that they can be understood by every one.—*The Interior.*

"If Mr. Edison's head is not turned by his numerous successes in wonderful discovery and invention, he must have a level head. Just as the announcement arrives, that the electric light is to be tested in the Capitol at Washington, a book is laid on our table, entitled "Edison and his Inventions," which, as the title implies, relates to the man as well as his work. It gives many interesting anecdotes of this odd genius, with full explanations of the telephone, phonograph, tasimiter, and last, and perhaps most important of all, the results of his electric light triumph. Numerous cuts make it comparatively easy for even the unscientific to understand the descriptive parts."—*Editorial in the Advance.*

"This volume of Mr. McClure's is one that will interest every reader. It is a graphic sketch of the incidents, anecdotes, and interesting particulars of his life. He gives a clear and concise explanation of the telephone, phonograph, and many others of the leading discoveries. The volume has many illustrations. Not only those older will read it with interest, but it is a book full of valuable instruction to the young, for its facts and for its suggestive thoughts."—*The Inter-Ocean.*

"There can be no doubt that Edison is a remarkable man. He has already accomplished more in the way of invention than any man on record, at so early an age—thirty-two. His career has been full of adventure, of a certain kind, and the story of it is exceedingly interesting. Mr. McClure has gathered his material with great industry, and so used it as to make a very readable book. An excellent idea is given both of the man and of his work."—*The Standard.*

"Mr. McClure has done a good thing in bringing together so much authentic information that relates to the man and his work. It is the story of the patient evolution of genuine talent, its discouragements and triumphs, with enough of personality to give additional zest to the narrative."—*Chicago Evening Journal.*

"Presents in an interesting manner the account of the life of the greatest inventor of the present time."—*Northwestern Christian Advocate.*

Sent by mail, post paid, on receipt of price by the Publishers.
Liberal discount to the Trade.

Motograph Receiver.

Telephonograph.

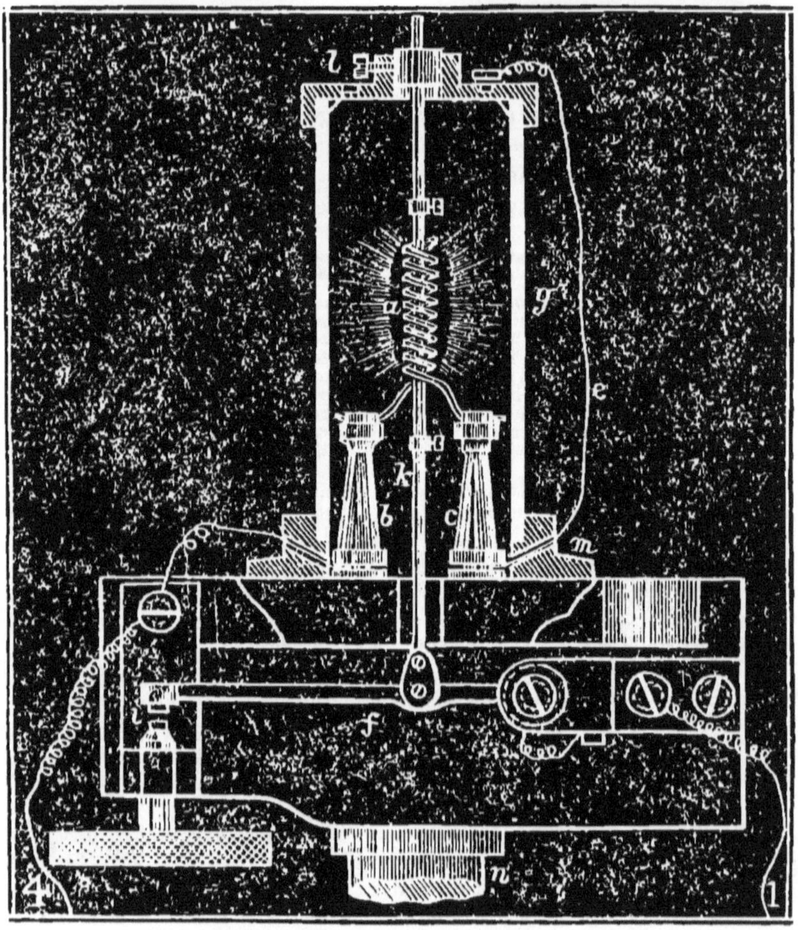

Edison's Electric Light.

Entertaining Anecdotes.

INCLUDING

Anecdotes of Noted Persons, Amusing Stories, Animal Stories, Love Stories, Falling Leaves.

FROM EVERY AVAILABLE SOURCE.

"*THAT REMINDS ME OF A STORY.*"

Edited by J. B. McCLURE.

8 vo 256 pages—Handsomely Illustrated. Price, in cloth, fine, $1.00 Paper cover, 50 cents. Sent by mail post-paid on receipt of price

RHODES & McCLURE, Publishers,

METHODIST CHURCH BLOCK, CHICAGO

Daniel Webster and the Farmer.

(From "Entertaining Anecdotes.")

Webster was out one day on the Marshes near Marshfield, busily shooting birds. It was a hot afternoon in August. The farmers were getting their salt hay on the marshes:

He came, in the course of his rambles, to the Green Harbor River, which he wished to cross. He beckoned to one of the men on the opposite bank to take him over in his boat, which lay moored in sight. The man at once left his work came over, and paddled Mr. Webster across the stream. He declined the payment offered him, but lingered a moment, with Yankee curiosity, to question the stranger. He surmised who Mr. Webster was, and with some hesitation remarked:

"This is Daniel Webster, I believe,"

"That is my name," replied the sportsman.

"Well, now," said the farmer, "I am told you can make from three to five dollars a day, pleading cases up in Boston."

Mr. Webster replied that he was sometimes so fortunate as to receive that amount for his services.

"Well, now," returned the rustic. "it seems to me, I declare, if I could get as much in the city pleadin' law-cases, I would not be a-wadin' over these marshes this hot weather, shootin' little birds."

FIFTIETH THOUSAND.

MOODY'S ANECDOTES

AND

ILLUSTRATIONS.

COMPILED BY REV. J. B. McCLURE, CHICAGO.

Comprising all of Mr. Moody's Anecdotes and Illustrations used by him in his revival work in Europe and America, including his recent work in Boston. Also, Engravings of Messrs. MOODY, SANKEY, WHITTLE and BLISS. Moody's Church, Chicago Tabernacle, Farwell Hall, etc.

OPINIONS OF THE PRESS AND EMINENT DIVINES:

"The wonderful sale of 'Moody's Anecdotes,' compiled by the Rev. J. B. McClure of Chicago, is the best evidence of the great value of this popular book. Thirty-four thousand copies have already been issued, reaching the seventh edition in three months. This is, perhaps, unparalleled in the history of Western literature; at least we know of no library book that has met with so large a sale in so short a time. It bids fair to sell right along, until everybody is supplied with a copy."—*St. Louis Evangelist*.

"'Moody's Anecdotes' is a handsome and handy volume, which many will prize as highly characteristic of the great Evangelist. Throughout its two hundred pages the truth is keenly applied by the aids of wit and a peculiarly vivid and pictorial pathos."—*New York Evangelist*.

"The book is handsomely printed and well compiled as to matter. It contains the pith of Moody's theology, methods and eloquence, and consists of a selection of the great preacher's best stories, drawn from his personal experience. It is a good insight into the workings and teachings of the great Evangelist and Christian Preacher."—*New Orleans Daily Democrat*.

"The incidents are related in character—it is Mr. Moody that speaks. They are short, pointed, peculiarly apt, as are all the illustrations of the Evangelist They form the arrows of the great marksman, and have done much of the execution of his sermons."—*Zion's Herald* (Boston).

"A book of anecdotes which have thrilled hundreds of thousands. During the last three months thirty-four thousand copies have been issued. Mr. McClure has done a good work in preparing this volume, which we commend to ministers, Sabbath-school workers and parents."—*Presbyterian Banner* (Pittsburg).

"It comprises the most striking stories, told in Mr. Moody's well-known concise and graphic style, and arranged in alphabetical order, according to the theme illustrated or set forth in the anecdote. The book has been compiled by Rev. J. B. McClure, whose scholarship and journalistic experience perfectly fit him to do the work discriminatingly and well."—*N. W. Christian Advocate* (Methodist).

"The book is handsomely printed, the matter is well classified, and will form an uncommonly interesting book. A capital book for the Sunday-school."—*Advance* (Congregational).

"Contains the pith of Moody's theology, methods and eloquence, all in one, and will be found agreeable for home reading and useful to the Sunday-school teacher and minister."—*Interior* (Presbyterian)

"Excellent reading, and by their brevity and point will be found especially good for that occasional and, perhaps, hasty reading, which is all that many persons can hope to find opportunity for."—*Standard* (Baptist).

"It is an attractive volume, including all the really interesting matter of Mr. Moody's discourses. A very valuable publication; is selling rapidly."—*Chicago Evening Journal.*

Price in Cloth, Fine, $1.00.   Paper Cover, 50 cts.

RHODES & McCLURE, Publishers, Chicago.

www.ingramcontent.com/pod-product-compliance
Lightning Source LLC
Chambersburg PA
CBHW030339170426
43202CB00010B/1181